UNDER THE GODDESS OF THE SKY

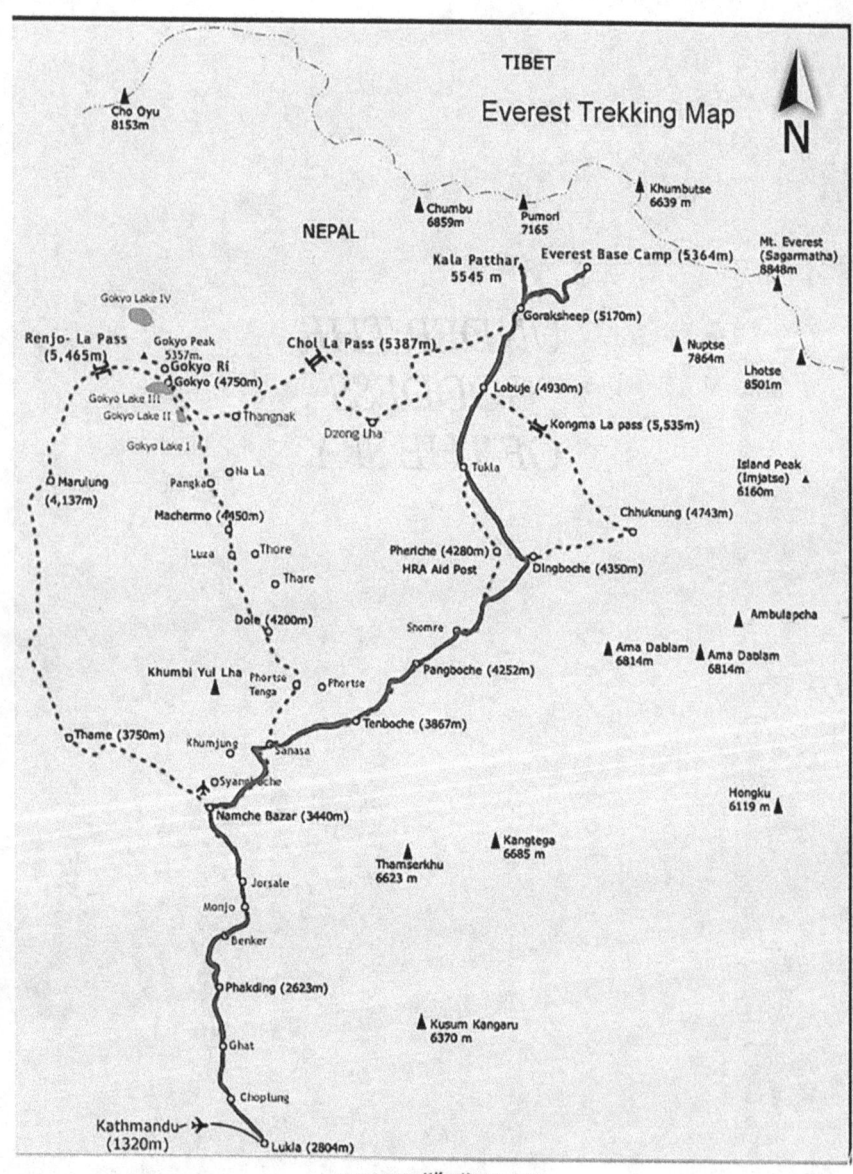

Under the Goddess of the Sky

A Journey Through Solitude, Bach, and the Himalayas

Judith Glyde

coffeetownpress
KENMORE, WA

A Coffeetown Press book published by Epicenter Press

Epicenter Press
6524 NE 181st St.
Suite 2
Kenmore, WA 98028

For more information go to:
www.Camelpress.com
www.Coffeetownpress.com
www.Epicenterpress.com

All rights reserved. No part of this book may be reproduced or transmitted in any form or by any means, electronic or mechanical, including photocopying, recording, or any information storage and retrieval system, without permission in writing from the publisher.

Unless credited, all photos and graphic drawings are those of the author.

Map of Everest Trekking Map, with permission: www.greattibettour.com

Pemba Sherpa in Eldorado Canyon, with permission: Sherpa, Pemba, with James McVey, *Bridging Worlds, A Sherpa's Story*, Sherpa Publications, 2019.

Johann Sebastian Bach **Six Suites pour violoncelle seul (Diran Alexanian)** Published by Editions Salabert, a catalog of Universal Music Publishing Classics & Screen, *International Copyright Secured. All Rights Reserved*, Reprinted by kind permission of Hal Leonard Europe BV (Italy)

Sherpa translations and script: with kind permission of Gelbu Goparma Sherpa

About the Author, photo credit and with permission, Roy Lewis

Under the Goddess of the Sky
2024 © Judith Glyde

Library of Congress Control Number: 2023951596
ISBN: 9781684921751 (trade paper)
ISBN: 9781684921768 (ebook)

Printed in the United States of America

Dedicated to Phuti and Chongba Sherpa,
and to their two girls, Mingma and Pasang,
for allowing this stranger to come into their home.
To dear friends, Tshering and Dinesh, my extraordinary guides,
and to Pemba Sherpa who convinced me to
bring the sounds of Bach to his home in Khumbu.

Dedicated also to my son, Jamie Glyde Lewis—a true individualist.
In my desire to be an adventurer in life,
he has been my inspiration.

Thank you – *Thuchhe*

My hope is that this volume will speak to a large audience: the adventurer, the musician, the travel enthusiast, the lover of mountains and all those in search of a challenge.

Any misrepresentations in the life of the Sherpa are strictly mine. In 1999 little had been written about the language and culture of the Sherpa. The 'why' to many of my questions could not be understood due to my minimal understanding of the Sherpa dialect; for me, this lack of the ability to communicate became the most consequential—the foundation of extreme isolation. Respecting the culture was of utmost importance to me, although, as an observer, I was wrestling with the dilemma of looking at the lifestyle and traditions of the Sherpa through the eyes of another's experience. I used my well-worn journal and photographs for memory, although I recognize that many details may be forgotten with the progression of time.

CONTENTS

Epigraph viii

PART 1 1
The Idea (*Rigpa* रिग्पा) 3
Arrival (Leyapsung लेयाप्सुंग) 6

PART 2 19
Beginning (*Gomsyokla* गोम्स्योक्ला) 21
Monsoon (*Yeru* येरू) 39
Traditions (*Doluka-Natang* डोलुक-नाताङ) 72

PART 3 85
Surrender (*Tong-jka* तोग जक) 87
Everest (chumolungma चुमोलुन्ग्मा) 102

PART 4 141
Returning Home (*Khangba Lokyi* खंग्बा लोक्यी) 142
Day Special 145
Conclusion (*Thedoma* थादोम्) 158

APPENDIX: Recipes from Phuti's Kitchen 163
MY SHERPA VOCABULARY 166
AUTHOR'S NOTES 168
ACKNOWLEDGEMENTS 171
REFERENCES 173
ABOUT THE AUTHOR 175

Epigraph

Those who are prepared to truly see and listen will find something different, and greater, than what they were seeking. They will find that the spirit and blessings of the mountains can be found, ultimately, within us all.

—Jamling Tenzing Norgay

PART ONE

THE IDEA
Rigpa रिग्पा

All seems to be moving at a snail's pace. Nepal, land of fabled Mount Everest, the snow and ice of the Himalayas, and my journey's end, is drawing near but only following three days of hours seeming like days—an eternity. The uncomplaining cello, an instrument that I have played for fifty years, has not produced a sound for a disgracefully long time, and I am struggling to go forward. Frightened does not begin to describe how I am feeling. I am fearful and anxious at what lies ahead; being apprehensive about the unknown is giving me an extreme case of cold feet. The cello and I are trundling along yet another tiled airport walkway, stepping on all variety of stairs and escalators, through security checkpoints, and with the rhythmic patter of the wheels on the cello case keeping me company—all with an extremely cumbersome backpack on very fatigued shoulders. Travelers on their own journeys stop to stare at the woman with too much baggage, and a few ask the questions, "What do you have in the case?" "Why does such a small person play such a big instrument?" I am accustomed to those queries and mumble a few words. All has been uneventful as the destination closes in, little by little. From Denver, Colorado, we made stops in LA, Tokyo, and Bangkok; and although appreciating the different cuisines offered by the airport eateries, the length of time was taking its toll. During the one overnight layover, I attempted to snooze on an extremely rigid metal airport bench with my cello tethered to my arm with a bungee cord; the backpack—my pillow;

luckily when I awoke, the cello and backpack had made it through the evening.

My flight on Thai Air from Bangkok is arriving in Kathmandu on schedule—the city being the second to last stop on this journey. It is the early afternoon of the third day. Dropping down through the low-lying cloud cover, I can see the urban sprawl that is the city—stretching for miles in all directions with low rooftops visible from horizon to horizon and a river seemingly splicing the city in half. As we drop closer, the architectural beauty of the sacred temples sharing space, Hindu and Buddhist, comes into view. My mind was seemingly playing tricks as I could imagine, hundreds of feet below, a Caribbean city bound by vegetation and stunningly picturesque hills. Having thought for months on end that I would be spending the next period in a land of snow and ice, I am taken by surprise at the greenness of the surrounding terrain. Looking past the features of the cityscape, however, I see the promised snow-covered peaks lining the hazy, bluish horizon. The mountains of the Himalayas are mysteriously close at hand and are beckoning me forward. In a few days I will be in their midst. Approaching the land of the million prayers, I have my own—that I will have the ability and understanding to carry through with what could be a most difficult quest, all things being considered.

As we make our final approach, I ponder the past few months. How did this all come about? The road to Kathmandu has been a long one. For those who know me well, there should be no mystery about the interconnections of ideas that have brought me to Nepal. I could have, of course, found a small cabin in the upper reaches of the Rockies to fulfill my ambitions; however, there was a flash of understanding for I knew what must be done. The profound essence of Bach coalescing with the majesty of some of the highest mountains in the world, the philosophy and meditation techniques of Buddhism that have been an interest for many years, and not in the least, my own nature—that of the searcher, the observer, the Romantic—for these reasons, I am in Nepal and about to spend three months with a Sherpa family in a land that is completely new to me. The only time I have been in Asia was for a performance in Almaty (Kazakhstan, in Central Asia) during a string quartet tour of the former Soviet Union. I am expecting a struggle because of what I assume will be an isolated, lonely journey through a musical rendering of my own self-portrait. If it will be necessary to sever ties with the usual, the customary way of living, it is not only predicted but anticipated.

I have been given an opportunity, thanks to my university in Boulder, to renew my relationship with the world of Bach, specifically the most renowned and august works ever written for the cello, the six cello suites—all the while living in the land of the Goddess of the Sky, the name not a mere epithet but in Nepali, *Sagarmatha* and in Tibetan, *Chomolungma*—both referring to Mount Everest.

After altering life-changes in the mid-point of my life, I believe that many questions, not only within myself but in the performance and teaching of these Bach suites, are unresolved. A truer, more mature connection with the suites will enable me to bring enlightenment to their musical pages, to myself, and for my students. As a Romantic, it has been easy to bring an idealized view of reality to the fore, believing as I do that the force and energy of the mountains in a land of meditation, spiritual and physical labor could embolden and invigorate the imagination. I wonder what I could discover if I met these suites again in the high mountains, in solitude, with no disruptions of modern living, and with all the time in the world. In short order, an amalgamation of these ideas came together: the causal agent (Bach), the highest mountains in the world for inspiration (the Himalayas), the world of meditation (Buddhism), and the solitude needed for self-reflection (in Khumbu). There was only one location that offered this opportunity; and, importantly, a place where absolutely no one could reach me—I am here.

I must put these thoughts aside for the time being for the wheels of the jet are touching down—we are landing. With fierce desire, I say to the listening gods, "please let this be a good day."

ARRIVAL
Leyapsung लेयापसुं

Exhausted and apprehensive, I tag along behind my fellow travelers as we exit the plane and make our way across the tarmac. After the days of climate-controlled airports and planes, the warmth of September in Kathmandu is intense; a wave of humidity and heat hits me as I head toward the airport entrance. Rolling the cello forward, I am thankful for its wheels; and even though I am wearing an awkward and overweight backpack (the cello clamps I packed have shifted in their position, and their rigid metal is digging into my spine), the heavy load is manageable. I enter the somewhat dilapidated and poorly lit terminal building and look for the signs to move forward. The crumbling facility suddenly magnifies the reality that Nepal is a developing yet economically and socially underprivileged country.

As I move through the noisy and raucous passageways with the other, very bleary-eyed passengers, my weariness does not prevent the sense of being in high alert, trying to be as attentive and responsive to my surroundings as possible. I am sure, merited by the looks I am receiving, that I am a strange sight pushing this large instrument, possibly musical although dead bodies have often been suggested, through the crowds. We come to a standstill at the airport security screening. Several officials are standing in front of a machine with a very crooked cardboard sign saying, "X-ray"—the sign written (in what looks to be crayon) with a surprisingly rudimentary handwriting. Another occasion in which I remember going through formal security in entering a country was at the Sheremetyevo Airport in Moscow. In that situation, in front of formidably stern officers, it was necessary for the personnel of the quartet to exhibit proof of ownership for their string instruments and bows. This was to substantiate that on our departure, we were leaving with our own instruments and with none belonging to the Soviet State. Trust is the key.

With the other passengers, I enter the short although slow-moving line for checking visas and passports. Thankfully, in my travels I have not misplaced any documents. Another step is completed; there is no problem with my visa and transit credentials. The official's demeanor, after appearing quite intimidating, becomes quite cheerful as he tells me that my two plane tickets to Lukla, the flight that will take me into the Khumbu region in three days' time (one ticket for me, one for the cello), are "not yet organized." I had followed the bizarre Nepali travel rule, one evidently purposed to keep track of my whereabouts: before I entered Nepal, since I would be leaving Kathmandu but remaining in Nepal, I had to notify the government regarding my plans. The authorities were to make the travel arrangements for me; and then, according to the rules, these forwarding travel tickets would be in the possession of this gentleman at the visa desk. With his cheerful smile and in fairly good English, he informs me that the tickets and authorizations to travel will arrive at my hotel that afternoon. This was a complication, hopefully not one of consequence; but at this moment it seems momentous, and not in a good way.

I am decidedly too tired, not to mention having difficulty concentrating, so I will take this information in good faith. Having the tickets in hand would have given me an indication that the next stage of my travel was assured. I have been trying to be positive—now, a slight wave of panic sweeps over me.

I collapse onto a nearby bench, hanging on to the familiar—the lifeline that is my cello. I just need a few minutes to collect my thoughts. In the airport I am to meet my guides, Tshering and Dinesh, who will help me in my transfer to the hotel and safeguard me through the coming days. They are friends of Pemba Sherpa, a person I met in Boulder when the seed of this adventure had barely germinated. I remember the day I met Pemba—a likeable fellow who was willing to give me advice about the Himalayas. Over lunch at a Nepalese restaurant, and after hearing of my desire to find a few months of solitude in the high mountains for the purpose of playing Bach suites, he suggested that I stay with his brother, Chongba, and his family in a small, isolated, Sherpa village, Sengma, on the side of a mountain at over 9,000 feet in the Khumbu region of Nepal (the region of Everest). In Sengma, there is no electricity, running water, or heat; he wondered if this would be alright. The cost was embarrassingly slight, and as he had mentioned the possibility of seeing Mount Everest in the same breath as isolation—agreement was immediately forthcoming. Several months later, sitting in the sweltering heat of the Nepali afternoon, the idea of no heat for the coming months was the least of my concerns.

The only thing on my overtaxed brain now is to leave the congested airport and make it to the hotel. All it would take is a welcoming bed as I am sure jetlag is settling in. I am hot and perspiring, anxious and feeling alone and with a definite sense of detachment. To overcome, I could attempt a brief conversation with others around me; however, I can honestly say that even a friendly and polite "hello" in Nepali would be stretching my communicative abilities at this moment. What is more, in the present circumstance I am too determined to find my two, hopefully friendly guides. I become very concerned as I make my way through the crowded entrance hall for I do not see my welcoming committee. With no one in sight that gives the impression of searching for me, I venture outside into the heat of late summer. I owe a debt of gratitude to probably Dinesh or Tshering as I notice a short, rather squat gentleman in a flowered shirt and shorts, holding a small sign with the words, 'Judith Glyde, Nirvana Hotel,' standing near a very diminutive, baby blue taxicab. With a grateful smile, I managed, "Namaskāra." Even though the cello, due to its size, looked to be not compatible with the dimensions of the vehicle, somehow the sympathetic driver managed to squeeze the instrument into the rear compartment as I slid into the front passenger seat.

We leave the complicated airport access roads and enter those of the outer city. Amidst the swelter and noise provided by sirens and the incessant honking of horns, the cab driver is keeping an angry, running conversation in Nepali with himself, presumably from what I can gather, referring to the frenzy in the streets. Even though the roads are unquestionably narrow, roughly paved and clearly one-way according to the street signs, the automobiles are nonetheless moving in both directions, sharing the passageways with pedestrians, the occasional pedaled rickshaw, and a cow or two. I do my best to take my mind far from the uproar, gazing at the many striking hues of the buildings, signs, and the profusion of goods hanging from the brightly-colored awnings of the outdoor street markets passing by. In the heat of the afternoon, I am delighting in the breeze wafting through the open car window. As we press on at a speed that is defying the conditions, the moment I ponder that perhaps people in the middle of the road should not have the right of way, we almost careen into several pedestrians, the driver slamming on the brakes. Holding on tightly and bracing myself (seatbelts were evidently not standard safety features), I am seriously thinking about having the driver make a U-turn (I am sure it would be legal) to return post-haste to the airport for an immediate return to the States. I am clearly wondering, "What in the hell was I thinking?" I know the answer to that question for I have always had a bad habit of coming up with an idea; and no matter how lacking in reason or feasibility, without thinking, I have pushed forward.

The problem now is that I know I am truly alone. Even the breeze, silenced for the moment, seems to have recognized a change. That I even conceive of being alone as a problem, in relative safety and with a good plan for the coming months, makes no sense. Along with my love of tall, silent yet energetic mountain peaks and the freedom they represent, I cherish the thought of the relative solitude they might be able to provide, the result of a natural inclination to be an attentive observer of behavior and daily life rather than being an active participant. The stories of Buddhist monks who squirreled themselves away for years in complete solitude before emerging out of their isolation to teach, some even in the austere sacred spaces of caves, have always been inspirational and provocative. In fact, when I first thought about Bach in the mountains, the Romantic artist's view of suffering and isolation was a possible way forward to bring new meaning to these works. To live in a Tibetan monastery within the stone walls of a 6x12' cell with only the sustenance of Bach and food slipped under the door was somehow appealing. A flight of fancy, perhaps, but at the time, incredibly enticing.

Now, riding in a Kathmandu taxi with the chaos and the resulting assault on the senses, the unknowns are perhaps taking on more importance than I thought possible. Even so, as I am trying to handle all of this by myself, I am fearful that I will not be able to conquer this uncharted territory. Rationally I know that any fear is short-lived for in the direst of circumstances, not to be overly dramatic, I have survived. In the same manner as this taxi ride, surrounded by dust and heat with my heart now beginning to pound and butterflies in my stomach, other challenges in the past have also been what I could call dire circumstances. In those moments it was necessary to defeat the nerves and anxiety that could have easily transformed themselves into a height of emotion difficult to soothe. The difference: in the past I have had others for strength and for overcoming fear. On every occasion of my life, I have had a support system which encouraged and motivated. In my growing years I had my family; throughout the time of my studies, I had fellow musician friends; and in my string quartet years I had my quartet colleagues. Finally, my friends at the university always gave the thumbs up to my ideas and endeavors. Even more than simple encouragement, as they recognized that this adventure was taking me to the land of the Sherpas and Buddhism, I was often met with a treasured affirmation: bowed heads and the folding of hands along with the whisper of the sacred syllables, "*Om, Om.*" They recognized my seriousness in this undertaking and seemed pleased to send me on my way.

Now, as I return my thoughts back to the chaos on the street, I think of the Buddhist *mantra*, "*Om mani padme hum*," literally meaning that "in dependence on the practice of a path which is an indivisible union of method and wisdom, you can transform your impure body, speech, and mind into the pure exalted body, speech, and mind of a Buddha."[1] The chant is known to be a calming phrase that can help to bring about peace of mind. I am driving into Kathmandu at the mercy of a regrettably disconcerting cab driver and with the absence of anyone who could relieve my doubts and to convince me that all will be well. The best move for me after considering the few options would be to turn around without any hesitation whatsoever.

I may be nervous and apprehensive, but I know why I am here. I cannot throw in the towel and concede defeat. There are many reasons why the route returning to the airport cannot be taken— the primary one being my confidence in the detailed preparation for every part of this astounding journey. There is no conceivable reason to give up at this moment in time. I know that spending three months in Nepal is a huge unknown, and that hardships will no doubt be unavoidable. I must become resolute in my desire to

---

1 "Dalai Lama, Kindness, Clarity, and Insight", *Snow Lion Newsletter*, Translated and edited by Jeffrey Hopkins and Elizabeth Napper, Autumn 2002.

take each moment in Nepal as it comes, trusting in my ability to solve any problem that materializes. I may be careening forward, literally, and figuratively, but I say to myself, "This is literally the first day and therefore, just the beginning." If I am to be honest, there is also no way this taxi can make a U-turn.

The little, blue taxi with its ranting driver and harried passenger continues to zip through crowded street markets and seemingly impassable intersections (two elephants, suddenly arriving with their drivers, are taking up too much space), entering what the driver called, with gesturing arms, the Thamel district of Kathmandu. In planning the trip, I knew that Thamel was the place to be. One of the oldest areas in this capital city, it has been known for years as a popular tourist district within Kathmandu. Within its streets I knew that the possibility of meeting others like me who wanted a little company was real. Now, past my window, I see a kaleidoscope of sight and sensory bombardment—every color imaginable mixing with the smells of rich Asian spices. On the crowded streets, now teeming with people rather than with vehicles, we pass shops that are advertising tour agents and trekking guides, money exchanges, stores, restaurants, cafes, and bars; and, looking into the maze of alleys branching away from the main roadway, I can see crudely constructed stalls selling everything imaginable keeping company with a wealth of temples and shrines. All this activity is catering to the immense number of tourists (mostly backpackers) that daily inundate the city.

Making our way through this crowded and colorful district, I disbelieve that the driver and I survived this mind-blowing drive from the airport. Owing a favor to the gods, we arrive at the Nirvana Garden Hotel. The entry into the parking lot is an arbor covered with multi-colored flowers announcing that the hotel is living up to its name. I had not only found a hotel with a garden, but a garden seemingly containing every conceivable species of the plant kingdom. The hotel entrance is adorned with more flowers, the building itself surrounded by green shrubbery and exotic-appearing plants. I look at the large, blue sign over the front door: NIRVANA; and I realize the synchronicity of this moment. There could be no better designation for my lodging in Kathmandu, for 'Nirvana' describes the goal of the Buddhist's path. I feel somewhat comforted.

Along with the sign, the facade of the four-storied structure affords quite a welcoming first impression, the feeling being one of a peaceful oasis in the tumultuous center of Thamel. On an outside terrace around the corner of the building, a few umbrella-covered tables and chairs are providing seating for several young men in western clothing—I assume, guests of the hotel. Angling my cello out of the back seat and grabbing my backpack, I paid the extraordinary yet heart-stopping driver the agreed-upon fee in rupees (roughly $1.00) and stepped into the lobby.

Thamel's reputation as being the main neighborhood and initial base for trekkers making ready to set out for the mountains is instantly confirmed as the reception desk, standing on the side of a warm, wood-paneled lobby, is overflowing with backpacks and trekking gear of all shapes and sizes—all spilling onto the floor and into the nearby seating area. Having held my breath for the past couple of hours, I can finally breathe. I am at a resting place for a few days. Pushing aside a few backpacks, I present myself at the desk. Two smiling and friendly faces greet me from behind the counter. The two women are beautifully dressed in traditional Nepali style— solid-colored pants with a long, beautifully patterned blouse. In addition, they both wore a beautifully colored scarf draped over their shoulders. They introduce themselves as Curry and Bizet. Not knowing how to really spell their names, I resort to a phonetic alphabet; no doubt, the spelling influenced by my appreciation of food and musical references. Again, as I found at the airport, my documents and advance booking reservation passed the litmus test. All seems surprisingly flawless. I nervously mention my flight to Lukla, "Will the tickets be arriving soon?" They assure me that they will keep an eye out for the travel documents. Another breath. A young, very smartly dressed boy with jacket and Nepali cap appearing to be about thirteen, arrives and grabs the cello and backpack, heading for the stairs. Unfortunately, my room is on the third floor; nevertheless, at the top of the stairs awaits a bed and a pillow. I follow, most grateful for the assistance.

Unbelievably, and to my surprise, I pass two American women who are speaking and gesturing energetically with some recent newcomers to the hotel. They ask about the cello. Familiar with giving short explanations to the question of 'why' I am travelling with the instrument, before long I find out that they have both recently graduated from the university in Boulder and are continuing to Tibet. The possibilities of meeting them, at this point in time and at this place, are totally, categorically bizarre. Their words, "You will love this hotel!" is sufficient for me to feel that I have made the best possible choice in selecting the Nirvana before beginning my journey into the mountains. I am going to be in Kathmandu for three days after which my adventure, hopefully not evolving into one with many more risks, will truly begin. Thankfully, anticipation and excitement are gradually having a needed effect—that of overcoming the apprehension that has consumed me during the past few days of constant travel.

Walking down a rather dim hallway and arriving at my room, I say good-bye to the young bellhop, giving him a few rupees for helping me. The brightly-lit room is incredibly small but full of promise as I see a twin bed with a white, woven bedspread and a pillow, both inspiring sleep. There are several decorative pictures on the walls devoted to several different Hindu deities along with beautifully patterned curtains and richly colored wall-hangings. The ambiance in the room is an effective reminder that I have finally arrived at the first destination in my three-month journey. I could care less that the maintenance person had left the room slightly less than perfect, with (I believe) a used cup and saucer on the bookcase. I am also taken aback with the number of little roaches on the decorative tile floor, not to mention several black flies buzzing around here and there. Nevertheless, I theorize that I am only at the hotel for a few days, and so much about the hotel is appealing and accommodating. Convincingly, I also believe that roaches are in the habit of remaining on the floor; and I don't believe roaches know how to fly.

I decide to investigate the cello, opening the case for the first time in ages to see if any damage had been caused to the instrument in the three days of making its way to Nepal. If there had been a chair on which to sit in the small, confined space (the springy, too soft bed would not do for this purpose), I would have played a few notes; instead, I spend a few seconds questioning for the thousandth time why I did not study the violin as standing, for that instrument, is a good alternative. But if I were a violinist, the Bach suites would not have been available to me, the work not being in the violin repertoire. As my cello gives every appearance of being in good condition (the strings have not snapped and are even in tune!), I delay producing a sound or two and collapse on the bed.

I am here. It has taken quite some time to put the components together for this venture—the who, what, when, why and how. These questions, however, became the components for a musical and physical journey, not for writing a good news story. Now that I have arrived in Nepal, I have a considerable amount of time to work on the causal agent: to discover if a different relationship with Bach, with the suites as the means of expression, is possible. The intention is not to necessarily transform my musical interpretations about the suites that have flourished in my psyche for many years in playing the compositions and learning from my cello colleagues, but to come to these treasured and revered works from a new set of circumstances—isolated and free from distractions. The intention is also to memorize the suites, hopefully to remember what has been forgotten over the years. All is designed not to relearn these suites just so that I can play a big concert or make a great recording—it is only for **me**. The ideas that I want to explore, ideas borne out of the desire to make new discoveries, are intriguing: what this land of the Sherpas and their way of living will bring to any new characterizations of these suites; what altitude may have in its effect, if any, on the sound I will produce; what changes from my earlier explorations will I make having to do with actual technique or with the reconstruction of the musical phrase; and, importantly, can I musically (and physically) thrive in isolation. To help me resolve these questions, I want to bring into this journey the Buddhist perspective of discipline and focus—a way of thinking I am eager to explore.

The idea that brought me here had its beginnings years ago, perhaps even back to my youth when my mother taught me Bach's first suite. The ensuing years studying the suites with Bernard Greenhouse and by association, with his teacher, Pablo Casals (the cellist who brought the suites into the light),[2] I tried to experience the essence, the expressive language of Bach—that Bach's language is one of communication other than with myself, like that of Buddhism. On one level, perhaps I have been successful. Years later, however, after an accumulation of experiences in my professional life, I believe that there is more to know. When I was younger and practicing the suites, they were exercises—a requirement in every student's repertoire. Now, I wonder what they can teach me. I want to discover in these suites (as the quest of the monk in his cave) a deeper connection—new discoveries that I can share with my students and to teach them a better, or different way to think about them. It is my hope that in bringing Bach to Nepal, I can give these works the kind of attention they deserve. As did Greenhouse and Casals, I believe that these suites can be understood by those who do not understand Western music. Perhaps bringing the music of an 18th century German Baroque composer to Nepal for study in relative isolation is not, after all, the result of completely irrational behavior.

Sleep not being on the agenda, and as I want to explore the area around the hotel before settling down for the evening, I make my way down the stairs and find what seems to be a user-friendly map of Thamel on the front desk that appears a trifle more self-explanatory than the map I had put in my pocket. The lobby door is thrown open, and I venture into the open air. And 'open air'

---

2   Clark, Andrew, "Pablo Casals and the Resurrection of Bach's Cello Suites", *Financial Times*, October 19, 2007.

it is. The light, temperate breeze of the late afternoon blows away the heat of the summer day. Standing in the entry, I breathe in the aromas of the garden, feeling for the first time a real sense of arrival. Before moving on, Kathmandu awaits.

PART TWO

PART TWO

BEGINNING
Gomsyokla गोम्स्योक्ला

I am eager to move forward; at the same time, I feel an incapability of making a considered decision. I am alone except for the two gentlemen still seated at the outdoor table, now having a rather heated conversation. As the walkabout depends upon leaving the hotel's entryway, I advance to the busy street in front of the hotel, now filled with bustling shoppers perusing the markets to find the bargains before suppertime. Turning right, I come to what appears to be a roundabout in the center of a main thoroughfare. I stop in my tracks. Automobiles and buses are at a standstill and at undecipherable angles. The only moving conveyances are the pedal-powered rickshaws and nimble motorcycles zipping through the traffic jam, sharing the roadway with pedestrians who have decided that the risk is worth it as they rush through the stationary cars and around the occasional cow. Speaking of cattle, they are sacred in this land as they are reincarnations of the goddess of wealth. Vehicles and pedestrians would normally pay attention to their whereabouts; for now, chaos reigns—the cattle could care less and lumber forward. Beyond any shadow of a doubt, rush hour is under way in Kathmandu. As I watch, the cars and buses gradually begin to creep ahead, trying to find a passage through the confusion. A thought comes to me that I am watching the scene of an action film, but without the star. Not wanting to plunge into the mayhem, I backtracked, returning to the hotel gate with life and limb intact. This road, one of the main streets through Thamel, seems to be busy yet fairly void of automobiles and less of a free-for-all. I can finally appreciate the sights as I join the shoppers on what appears to be primarily a pedestrian roadway, walking slowly and taking the time to examine and explore the busy and picturesque area. Only beautifully decorated rickshaws, bicycles, and a sporadic motorbike move along with the shoppers. Considering the variety of shops catering to the backpacking industry, this street appears to be the main trekkers avenue that is highlighted in all descriptions of Thamel.

The shops situated on both sides of the paved but narrow roadway are decked out in colorful flags. They are open for business, many with their goods hanging from the make-shift stalls in front; their signs being invitations to enter. As dusk is fading, lights have been turned on; in addition, some incandescent lamps crisscross the roads, announcing the beginning of Thamel's nightlife. The shops and some residential buildings, primarily one- or two-story establishments, seem to be constructed in a conglomeration of materials (brick, old stucco, wood) mirroring the "everything but the kitchen sink" mix of goods sold on the streets below. Not only the structures, but the clothing worn by those in the street is an amalgamation of style—a vivid assortment of traditional ethnic combined with western modern. As one would expect, the older men and women are in the traditional, the younger gravitate to the trendsetting and stylish jeans and t-shirt. The outdoor clothing markets, often taking up a great deal of space in the street, are selling a wide assortment of multi-colored merchandise: t-shirts advertising the latest pop band or clever designs, sweaters of yak wool, cashmere scarves, rugs, and wearables of all types. Overhearing one bargaining Englishman, I observe that all can be purchased for very little. A car comes through, honking its horn incessantly, disrupting the activity in the street for a moment. After it passes, I continue my stroll through the lively, jostling crowd with pop music blaring in discordant harmony from several adjoining bars. Above, in close juxtaposition, signs hawk for massage parlors and spas for tired travelers, ATM machines, laundries, trekking and tour companies, bakeries, and food, food, and more food. I have never seen so many restaurants and cafés in one limited location, and the smells! There was a moment when one odor was indistinguishable from the next: fruity, pungent, sweet, woody—all is compressed into olfactory confusion.

Only two minutes from the hotel, I discovered the little Pilgrim's Bookstore, a store that has been No.1 on my list to locate. Not to be believed, on a separate shelf with maps and guidebooks, I chance upon a very small language dictionary. More like a pamphlet, it seems to list important words and phrases in Sherpa with the equivalencies in Nepali. As the Sherpa language is basically a spoken and not written dialect, it was extraordinarily difficult in Colorado to find any sort of publication with Sherpa words and their translations. Discovering this little publication, I may have a head start on communication when I arrive in Sengma, at least I can only hope. Along with my dictionary purchase, I found a perfect writing journal—one beautifully crafted in Nepal with handmade paper. My goal will be to keep a day-to-day account of the daily trials and triumphs—hopefully an inordinate amount of the latter, and few of the former.

Proud of myself for my new acquisitions along with feeling quite 'in charge' (I am recognizing some of the eateries and shops from my months of map research and reading), I begin to hunt for someplace to have dinner. Before leaving Boulder, thinking I might need to hear a familiar voice after arriving in Nepal, I had made a quick study of the popular haunts where English-speaking tourists found company and food, and where trekkers could find good conversation and advice. Today I have been so concerned and anxious with everything around me, I have thought little about the usual, important activities, such as having something to eat. On the right, I pass by the Blue Note Café, wondering if it is a jazz club; and if it is related in some way to the famous nightspot in New York City's Greenwich Village (the memory of Stan Getz and his trio playing there in the late 60's is with me still). I eventually found what I have been looking for—the Northfield Café & Jesse James Bar. The sign above the entrance announces its dual name and the type of food being offered: American, Mexican, Indian, and Continental. The Northfield, with its checkered tablecloths, small tables, and warm atmosphere, is a café that is a famous and popular trekker hangout, no doubt because of the variety of offerings. I order a pizza, an offering on the menu even though the café has neglected 'Italian' in its advertising. My choice of a simple, marguerita pizza has clear reasoning: because it is assembled and placed immediately into a hot oven there is less chance of my becoming ill. I am definitely keeping in mind that Kathmandu is known to be a food poisoning trouble spot for tourists, especially with street food and in some questionable restaurants. An illness now, at the very beginning of this journey, would be disastrous.

One such experience has stayed with me for years, tempering my relationship with all food that has the appearance, taste, or smell of being remotely questionable. In the early 80's, my string quartet was in San Miguel de Allende, Mexico, performing at the Belles Artes Music Festival. My son, Jamie, ate some peaches canned by a Canadian artist friend then living in San Miguel. As the canning process involves a great deal of boiling, I thought it would be safe for him to eat. Jamie became so ill and felt so badly that at age four he wrote a will, leaving all his worldly goods to his friends.

Reminded of this incident, I must be careful. Even though the bottle of water on the table is tightly capped, I am assuming that my water purifier will come in handy after I arrive in Sengma. Putting negative food thoughts aside, tonight at the Northfield in Thamel the pizza is delicious and clearly with a Neapolitan character in taste. I could say that it is almost indistinguishable from a pizza one would order at the Antica Pizzeria in Naples, or perhaps I am just starving. In any case, this traveler approves.

While at the Northfield, I talk to a few hikers who are leaving at the end of the week for the Annapurna circuit—treks in the mountains of central Nepal. This is an area of Nepal that I had considered when planning this trip but meeting Pemba and knowing that I would have a chance to see Everest made my decision about the Khumbu region, easy. I also found out that unbelievably, at the airport this morning, a few hours before my plane landed, a small aircraft arriving from Pokhara (in Annapurna) had crashed on landing in Kathmandu after hitting a telecommunications tower, the crash killing all 15 aboard.[3] My anxious level having risen, slowly I walk back to the hotel in a bit of a fog. The activity in the street has not diminished in the least. For me, the excitement in the air refutes the tragedy of a short while ago. Shops are still open, many hikers with backpacks on their shoulders sauntering down the street, conversation is loud and raucous, and the feeling of camaraderie is in the air—the catastrophe perhaps bringing everyone together. With my purchases, the Sherpa language book and the journal, I arrive back at the Nirvana. My plane tickets to Lukla, along with the document permitting my travel outside Kathmandu, are at the desk. Everything has arrived. I suppose I have assumed that nothing is going to work well for me in Nepal; but I am, for the moment, wrong. Plans are taking shape, and I will try to relax. Sleep comes easily as my head hits the pillow—I am just too tired to think about the air travel coming up…and roaches be damned.

The next morning, I discovered the most significant drawback of the room—hot water in the shower is variable. The heat must come and go according to its own schedule. This morning it is non-existent. Making do with a cold shower, I follow the smell of fruity yet strong coffee and find that the Nirvana has quite a pleasant restaurant alongside the lobby. Perhaps the hot drink and food will make up for the chill upstairs. Soon after my breakfast of coffee and sweet fried dough (a traditional Nepalese dish made with rice flour, *sel roti*), I finally met Tshering and Dinesh. A young couple enters the restaurant and, with cheery smiles, the two introduce themselves—Tshering is Sherpa and Dinesh, Nepali. Living in Kathmandu, a short distance from the center, they arrived at the

---

3 Jeziorski, Andrzej, "Nepal suffers second fatal crash", *Flight Global*, September 14, 1999.

hotel to go over plans for the next leg of the trip. Effusive in their apologies for not meeting me at the airport, before anything else they presented me with a white greeting scarf, a *kata*. Giving a scarf to a newcomer is a beautiful Nepali custom which, in my case, will give a positive tone to my journey. Even though Pemba had only given me the briefest of introduction to this couple, because they speak English and are so enthusiastic about my visit to Kathmandu and to Sengma (they cannot wait to see and hear me play), I am positive that they will be delightful companions for the next few days and will be quite able to ease my continuing apprehension—my new "best friends" in a foreign land.

The plan they outline seems unproblematic, even if challenging. Tshering is planning to join me on the flight to Lukla, helping to translate if needed at the airport and, once we arrive, in finding a sherpa to carry the cello to Sengma. This trek entails climbing down a mountain, crossing over a river, (the Dudh Kosi, the main waterway coming down from Everest) and climbing back up to Sengma. Before the trek, after arriving in Lukla, we are going to make our way a short distance north to the village of Chaurikharka where Tshering's family lives. As she has not seen her mother and stepfather for some time, she is looking forward to a short visit. I am thankful that I found the little Sherpa dictionary but having Tshering with me for the first day of introductions in Lukla and Sengma will be a godsend. Dinesh will be staying in Kathmandu as he works for a company (internet, I believe) that keeps him extremely busy. He will be forwarding any email or posts for me, any correspondence travelling to Lukla and then on to Sengma.

Chatting with Tshering and Dinesh on this first full day in Kathmandu, and perhaps hoping for some calming words, I mention the tragedy that had happened the day before. (Note to self: it can be unproductive behavior to take to heart every discussion that swirls around me.) If a plane had crashed coming into a rather large airport that is Kathmandu, what would happen to a really small plane flying into the airstrip at Lukla? Not only listening to others, I should also be careful about what I read. I remember a description of the landing at Lukla that I had read months ago—one I should not have read let alone remembered. It is probably not even worth mentioning for most have survived the experience.

What I had read was the following: The airstrip at Lukla is short, handling only small aircraft. "It is a tricky place to land a plane because everything is down to the judgment of the pilot with no radio beacons for guidance and no second chances once the pilot is committed to land. The pilot appears to aim into the lower end of the runway, pulling up at the last minute. This looks rather alarming from the passenger compartment as you dive into the mountains, then onto the runway hurtling towards the rock wall at the end of the airstrip. The landing is rough and bouncy since little is done to maintain the airstrip. Not surprisingly there've been some accidents."[4] As I do not love flying especially in small planes, tending to imagine a possible disaster at the slightest hint of turbulence, and being aware that flying into Lukla was soon to be in my future, I wonder why I had read that article. After I mentioned the Pokhara plane, adding that I had heard the landing at Lukla airport was not a great experience, Dinesh decided to elevate the level of my anxiety by giving me even more information: that the Lukla runway is unpaved, that it has an almost 12% incline (the slant being helpful in aiding a quick stop, necessary to avoid the mountain dead ahead), and the clincher—that it has been named the most dangerous airport in the world for quite a few years.[5] Tshering adds, "Don't worry; all will be well." I am determined to be stoic and not transmit my true feelings no matter how nervous I am to take that flight. I have a feeling that from this moment on I am going to be living in a continuous state of anxiety.

Tshering and Dinesh must leave for a few moments to make a phone call at the front desk. I am bewildered and am trying, unsuccessfully, to keep my positivity level up. It is even more disconcerting because having traveled around the world performing and teaching with the quartet I should be used to the

---

[4] McGuinness, *Trekking in the Everest Region*, 147.
[5] In 1999, the runway was a dirt track; it was paved in 2001.

vagaries of travel. Being in extraordinary conditions (wiretaps, unwanted overnight stays) I have always been able to put things in perspective. Even after the joy of feeling a sense of equilibrium last night as I roamed the streets of Thamel, I continue to doubt the logic of this adventure. I wonder if I am up to the task—not of Bach but of the precariousness of it all. My curiosity about what lies ahead—in the possibilities, will push me onward. The spirit of inquiry is what brought me here. I will have to accept that the paradoxical feelings of indecision and courage will have to remain.

For this journey I have arranged as much as possible, but there still seems to be a great deal that feels in the 'unknown zone.' When traveling, especially abroad, I always consider any what-ifs imaginable. I once drove down the eastern coast of Italy by myself to see the sights along the incredibly picturesque Adriatic coast. I had planned how many miles I would drive each day, the hotels with contacts and directions, and the scenic and historic places I wanted to visit. Some would say this was a bit of overkill as I was not allowing for the unexpected experience—gone was improvisation. However, in lieu of friends or family for assurance, this is how I proceed when by myself. Interestingly, this type of planning beforehand is similar to the preparation for a concert. The difference lies in the afterward: once the hard work has been concluded with every musical detail considered, the sense of improvisation is free to take over. Only then am I able to communicate, to share intimate thoughts with an audience. Where is that improvisation now when I need it?

Tshering and Dinesh return, and I put those thoughts aside. For this first day in Kathmandu, Dinesh is offering to be my guide. I would love to absorb as much of the vitality, vibrancy, and history of this city as possible for I am assuming that after I arrive in Sengma with only Bach for company, my days in comparison will be rather quiet.

I have come to Nepal with the portrait of the Buddhist teacher in contemplative isolation being the inspiration. As the premise of this entire journey, the idea is rather remarkable as I feel that I know so little about the philosophy of Buddhism itself. And yet, even as a novice, I want to draw on some of its precepts to bring more of a direct insight into myself and in so doing, more insight into Bach and his music. Here I am in Kathmandu, a World Heritage Site, surrounded by a few thousand temples and monuments—sacred religious locations both Hindu and Buddhist. The opportunity to learn something more is phenomenal. To that end, I propose visiting three spiritual temples (*stupas*) in the area: the Buddhist Swayambhunath and Boudhanath Temples, and Pashupatinath, the most revered Hindu temple in Nepal. Dinesh, agreeing with the plan but with a mind to improvisation (!), suggests that we first walk to the hub and the heart of Kathmandu, Basantpur or Durbar Square (it is also purposeful, as we must pick up his car). I want Dinesh to think of me as a tourist—I want to follow along and learn.

Leaving Tshering behind, Dinesh and I walk from touristy Thamel to the narrow back streets—some roughly paved, some unpaved, the latter dusty and dirty. Chickens are searching for food, and the occasional dog is stretched out and resting on the road as we pass. One would think that in the alleyways and side streets the atmosphere would be marginally more peaceful; but there are the inevitable outdoor markets, rickshaws and motorbikes with their passengers, and the proverbial cacophony of honks, bells, and beeps from every conceivable type of moving vehicle.

After strolling along for about twenty minutes, we come to the outskirts of the Royal Square. These courtyards and temples once belonged to Nepal's Royal Family—a site associated with coronations and festivities from ages past. Struck with a profusion of aromas that together are difficult to identify (incense with perhaps turmeric and marigolds), we pass through a paved, open-air market filled with street vendors and marigold sellers; stalls selling statues, wooden flutes, clothing, scarves, and bowls of all sizes; and trinket sellers with their goods exhibited on mats—all in competition for the passerby. Surrounding the square proper are many alleys and side streets lined with temples, more souvenir shops, and cafes with local food—the latter is a temptation with the promise of a Nepali espresso, yet now is not the time. Happily, the square itself is bare of automobiles and the resulting chaos. Along with pedestrians and monks, I see only the occasional motorbike, a few bicycles laden with fruit, and rickshaws, unfortunately with their incessant bellringing. Two elephants with their riders amble along—not an unusual sight to those who inhabit the square, for this area had been the royal elephant stables many years ago. After we take a few moments to watch the activity, the commotion fades from sight and hearing. I can now concentrate on the beauty of the structures before me. There are approximately fifty temples in Durbar, but many are out of sight. I am looking at quite a few, nonetheless. Surrounding the temples and in the niches and porches of the structures are vibrant multi-hued sculptures of Hindu gods and goddesses. Multitudes of live birds line the edges of the projecting gables, one roof above another in the pagoda-style. The entrances are embellished with painted wood carvings and decorative statues with a wash of color that is extraordinary. Durbar Square is a holy Hindu location—not Buddhist. Even though most of the Nepalese population is Hindu, both Hindu and Buddhist religions have existed in Nepal since recorded history. If this square is just the beginning of our scenic and historic tour today, I am in awe of the sights and sensations of this first act.

We locate Dinesh's car just outside of the square. Being a passenger once again in an automobile thrust into the confusion and mayhem that exists on a Kathmandu roadway, I am reminded of yesterday's trip from the airport. Dinesh is thankfully not ranting and raving as the harried taxi driver had done, in fact he is very calm. Like the cabbie, he is also a master at avoiding everyone and everything on the road. The air conditioning is appreciated as the weather has become very oppressive and humid. The traffic gradually subsides, becoming less disorderly as we approach the Swayambhunath Temple, also known as the Monkey Temple—a most sacred Buddhist religious site.

Leaving the car, after a short walk we arrive at a set of stairs leading up to the temple— a staircase that I have read about, the

'365 Stairs to Illumination.' Walking up these steps, one for each day of the year, will give me the opportunity to reflect on the importance of the passing of each day. At the base of the stairs is a grand, multicolored Buddha statue. A young girl sits alongside Buddha to rest before the climb. More small monuments, Buddhas, and *stupas* line the stairway—a veritable extravagance of color surrounding us as we begin the ascent. As each step passes by underfoot, I offer a prayer entreating that each day that passes in Sengma will give me the peace and calm for which I am striving in this journey.

As we trek steadily up, I cannot help but realize how grateful I am for understanding, months ago, that being in good physical shape was integral to the success of this trip and essential to my state of happiness. Having functioned for some time at more than a mile above sea level, I assumed that the years I had spent at altitude would be more than helpful in acclimatizing myself for existing and hiking in Nepal, not to mention avoiding the headaches and dizziness of altitude sickness. Nevertheless, in preparation for this journey, I spent as many waking hours as possible hiking the steep and challenging hills behind my home.

Halfway up the 365 steps, I am still breathing. The higher we climb, chanting from the summit grows in intensity; and by the time we reach the top, Nepali string music and drums have joined the loud clamor. When the stairs finally end, we are surrounded by the prerequisite shops and stalls. Souvenirs are being sold on every corner amidst a strong smell of candles and incense. Trying not to spend too much time thinking about the tourist element, I focus my attention on the magnificent, white-domed *stupa* with the gold tower and spire at the top and prayer wheels circling its base. The painted eyes of the Buddha at the lowest part of the tower, the eyes denoting compassion and wisdom, look down upon us. I stand for a moment pondering this temple—Buddha expressing concern and sympathy for humanity's suffering. The rainbow colors of many Buddhist prayer flags are spilling along the sides of the temple from the top of the spire to the bottom of the dome, the flags in company with numerous monkeys scampering all over the temple walls. I have almost forgotten about these little creatures and why they are commanding such attention. This temple is, after all, known as the Monkey Temple due to the macaques, a famous species of monkey that has lived in the northwest part of the temple complex for generations.

Before we leave the temple grounds we move clockwise around the *stupa* (clockwise, mirroring the movement of the sun across the sky), turning the many prayer wheels covered with Buddhist mantras that surround the base.

From this height, the view that looks over Kathmandu is extraordinary. It gives a birds-eye view of the cityscape surrounded by the mountains in the distance. Walking through the nearby outdoor market, the macaques brush against our ankles. The seemingly friendly animals are asking for food of any kind. A couple, tourists in shorts, are agitated around them, using their voices and hands to keep them away. Dinesh tells me that the monkeys have been known to bite visitors in their demand for food, but we escape unscathed. After the awe-inspiring view at the top of the hill, the downward steps back to the car—effortless.

We now drive eastward, moving through a city that seems unduly quiet (perhaps it is lunchtime). Arriving at the Pashupatinath Temple on the banks of the river Bagmati (the waterway that was 'splicing the city in two'), I find myself casting aside the joyous feeling of Swayambhunath, replacing the feeling with the heavy atmosphere of Pashupatinath, a site dedicated to the god Shiva. Hundreds of elderly followers of Hinduism arrive at the temple each year to find a resting-place for the last few weeks of their lives—to meet their death, to be cremated on the banks of the river, and to travel their last journey on the Bagmati. Some who come to this place believe that if they die in the temple, they will be reborn as human beings. I can only look at the site from across the river as only Hindus can enter the main temple complex. The temple itself, in the middle of the network of buildings, is a magnificent structure. The temple is in a pagoda-style architecture with a tiered gold-plated roof adorned with red valances, and with steep golden steps approaching the entrance. In the complex, Dinesh tells me, there are temples and shrines amidst a dense, concentration of structures, all covered with intricate carvings and sculptures. As chimes tinkle in the small breeze and the smell of juniper incense blossoms, I turn to view the sight along the Bagmati. On the sides of the river but on the temple grounds, I see several fires burning on raised platforms that have been built for the funeral pyres. A man, on one of these platforms, is occupied in his livelihood, brushing the ashes into the river. There is much sadness along the Bagmati this afternoon. People are mourning, saying goodbye to their loved ones. Not much is said as we walk back to the car.

We drive, only a couple of miles, to Boudhanath. All is smooth going—rush hour will not begin for a few hours. Chaos will then reign, yet again. Dinesh is telling me about his life and work in Kathmandu, and how he would love to visit America. Our conversation is cut short as after only a few minutes we can see the temple—a mammoth structure. We park and then walk until the temple is before us. Surrounded by a white wall filled with hundreds of prayer wheels, the temple is in the center of a plaza, the plaza circled by a grey, paved path, the path surrounded by a red, dirt and worn track. We, in turn, are surrounded by color: flags, shrines, shops, and markets. Color, along with its vitality, is the heart and essence of this city. Hearing the clanging of bells (of all tones and intensity) and the music of drums and flutes, I feel included along with the pedestrians and worshippers in the hustle and bustle around me. Boudhanath Temple, a beacon of Buddhist belief and the holiest Tibetan Buddhist temple outside of Tibet, is one of the largest *stupas* in the world. It towers over the city and is said to have been created after the passing of the Buddha. The temple is inlayed with Buddha images; its painted eyes, on all sides of the tower base, keep watchful gaze in every direction. I must admit, the eyes do seem to be looking down upon us and rendering judgement as well as comfort. As at Swayambhunath, Buddhist prayer flags fly from top to bottom. Bells on the inside of the walls are constantly being rung, fusing with the sound of chants in both muffled and discernible tones. Dinesh and I join with those who are intoning softly and carrying Tibetan prayer beads in the pilgrim 'way,' going clockwise (the '*kora*') around the large circumference of the structure and turning the many wheels. The legend is that if you go around the perimeter with only positive thoughts, you will only receive good karma. As I circle the temple, thinking about what is ahead and the interconnection between my journey and the sacred sites we have visited today, I try to focus on as many constructive and affirmative sentiments as possible.

As we return to the car, in the grounds around the *stupa*, we pass hundreds and hundreds of birds being thrown buckets of seed by those apparently tending the feathered creatures. The aromas of spices and burning wood emanating from the neighboring cafes remind us that we are hungry—it is time for lunch. This day of memories, with its vibrant introduction to Nepal's history and culture, will be one I take with me to Sengma. I feel certain that the passion I absorbed today from the faithful, the adherents to both Buddhism and Hinduism, will further sustain me as I search for my own enlightenment in the days ahead.

Looking forward to something to eat, we returned to Thamel to meet Tshering for a mid-afternoon lunch. We decided to try an historic restaurant within walking distance of the hotel. Incredible aromas are wafting out of the kitchen of the Roadhouse Café (not a lodge nor a nightclub)—the burning of wood and sauteed onions are the two distinctly identified. It is wonderful how the thought of food brightens the senses and can cause such joy! *Momos* (steamed dumplings), vegetable curry with rice and lemongrass tea are ordered as soon as we sit down. I had read about the Nepali eating, as is their custom, with the fingers of their right hand. Being an 'outsider' and no doubt as a courtesy, I am given a spoon—it is highly appreciated. No further mention of disasters ensued; we spoke only of Kathmandu and Sengma. Dinesh and Tshering are ready to show me more sights, but I beg off feeling the need to restore myself after the morning spent in the city. Tomorrow, they will leave me to relax; the following day we leave for Lukla. The fateful moment of truth is presenting itself.

Before I leave for the mountains, there is one more thing that I cannot neglect for it may not be possible anytime soon. Asking a gentleman at the front desk to dial New York, I call my son. Jamie must have been amazed to answer his phone to hear a voice say, "Namaste, Nepal is calling." When we spoke, he asked one question, "is it incredible?" I believe, after telling him that I seriously pondered the idea of coming home instead of continuing with this adventure, he could tell that I am a bit disorientated. Nevertheless, he understands that I will follow through to the end. Before we say goodbye, he has as usual, the perfect words of encouragement, "Mom, you always make things happen—not quitting is our joint nature. You can do it."

Even with those comments, I am coming to grips with being out of my comfort zone in Nepal. Thinking about the plane that did not make it and Lukla being a dangerous airport, I cannot avoid the concern and anxiety. One calming thought: on the day I leave Kathmandu, Dinesh and Tshering will be leading me through the next hurdle.

The next day I roamed the streets, poking my head into a shop or two and enjoying what seems to be a fusion of Indian and Tibetan food. I don't have an adventurous palate, so I stuck with the familiar *momos* and *dal bhat*. Rain began after I returned to the hotel; the sound of the water splashing against the window had a tranquillizing effect—I fell asleep quickly. Waking in the morning, the rain has become a slight drizzle. I wonder if this is the last 'hurrah' of the monsoon season, a topic of conversation at the Northfield two days ago. Having seen so many trekkers in the city and knowing that the climbing weather in the high mountains begins in the fall after the heavy rains have ended, I am hoping Nepal is experiencing the monsoon's swan song.

The day to leave Kathmandu has arrived. After another cold shower, I pack quickly. Bringing my cello and backpack with me, I head downstairs for breakfast. I am alone as Tshering and Dinesh will meet me at the airport. The woody and cedar smell of the coffee greets me; I order a cup right away. It is strong but exactly what is needed. Another order of *sel roti*, and I am prepared and ready to go.

I asked Bizet to please request a taxi. As the clouds have lifted, and as the cab will materialize in roughly twenty minutes, I spend the time in the outside garden of the Nirvana, relaxing with the vibrancy and fragrances of the flowers on the deck: orchids, red rhododendrons, and orange marigolds are almost garish in color. The taxi arrives. It is a black sedan with significantly more space than the cab from the airport; as a result, the driver and I, along with the cello, fit nicely (no cramming necessary). On this occasion the return to the airport is without any chaos; in addition, the driver is singing along to a Nepali tune on the car radio. In general, the ride feels rather calm and pleasant. There is restraint on my part to hold any conversation due to my active seeking of inner peace. As we approached the airport, morbidly I tried to spot the remains of the plane that had crashed. Luckily, this effort is to no avail. Leaving the taxi and preparing to join the probable disorder in the terminal, I see Tshering and Dinesh waiting for me in the entrance. Dinesh says goodbye and good luck for he must return to work; he will be seeing me when I return to Kathmandu. Agonizingly, those three months seem like decades in the future. Tshering and I experience smooth passage through the requisite visa and security desks; this time, however, I let her take care of the paperwork. We ask at the gate and discover that there is a two-hour delay due to bad weather in Lukla. Are they kidding? Have I neglected to mention how much I hate flying? I return to the seeking of inner peace, unfortunately finding meditation is not being successful. My anxiety is palpable.

Having Tshering by my side, however, gradually calms and diminishes my nervousness. We find a quiet spot in a corner of a nearby café and chat about her family home in Chaurikharka over a cup of *llam*, a popular tea with the familiar taste and smell of Darjeeling. The two hours go swiftly by, and soon we head out on the tarmac to board a rather small Yeti Airlines plane, with two pilots sitting up front. The aircraft is carrying about twelve-thirteen trekkers, male and female, all excitedly speaking as they try not to think about the flight ahead. The Lukla airport and its reputation is evidently known to all. In addition, I know some of my fellow passengers are about to face dangerous situations as they trek northward. Their smiles and joyful demeanors bely that fact but cause me to silently wish them luck. Backpacks of all sizes join my cello in the aisle due to miniscule overhead compartments and a too-small baggage area. The explanation that I have a ticket for the cello (although the large case had a fat chance of fitting into the narrow seat) evidently did not translate into Nepali; nor, I doubt, did the pilots want to say "no" to another ticketholder. Tshering is probably thinking it quite humorous that I have this extra ticket for what appears to be simply baggage. The idea of the cello being in the aisle is slightly frightening, although I must say it is one of the easiest handlings of the instrument in a plane of any size in my memory. I would love to see the cello lying in the aisle of a Boeing 727; I would also love to see the fortune I could have saved in tickets.

In my thirty years of having to cope with trying to explain why I have a ticket for the cello, having the cello in the aisle is, for a short trip, not a bad idea at all. In America, a flight attendant not acknowledging that musical instruments the size of a cello can legally hold a ticketed seat is known to all cellists in their travels as the most significant hurdle to overcome, especially in the United States. These instruments are just too expensive to be put below in baggage. FAA regulations, attempting to be accommodating, stipulate that a cello must go in the bulkhead on a specific plane and by a window (not all planes, though, have bulkheads). I have had cello friends that once on board a plane holding a ticket with the correct conditions met, claim to the flight attendant (after he/she feloniously argues that a cello is too large and must go below in baggage), that the case contains a *balalaika*. As this instrument is Russian and is not known to those who penned the FAA regulations, the attendant will let the *balalaika* take its seat. One does what one needs to do.

In this specific case, on the Yeti plane, having the cello in the aisle unrestrained with all the backpacks, was a definite first. As the Yeti plane prepares to take off for Lukla, Tshering shares with me that even after the two-hour delay, there may be difficulty landing in Lukla due to a report of high winds, cloud cover and bad visibility. She adds, "Don't worry, Judith, it is dangerous because the pilots have no beacon to follow, but they have received the proper training." Remembering that I forgot to tell Tshering that expressing every thought was unnecessary, I cross my fingers—a small physical act that soothes the knot in my stomach.

Underlying it all, the word 'frisson' is a good descriptor of my inward feeling, not unlike riding the roller coaster on Coney Island—the meaning of the word lying directly between thrill and fear. I must somehow relax in the knowledge that this journey with solitude, Bach and the Himalayas is just the next stage of my life's reality. If life is the preparation for death in the Buddhist tradition, I want to experience all that life has to offer before the ultimate manifests itself. The plane begins to taxi, the engines roar, and we are off. The next stop: Khumbu.

MONSOON
Yeru येरू

We take off with a roaring of the engines and the high-pitched, singing tone of the propellers. Once alight, balls of cotton wool are given to us for our ears as the engines are extremely loud, making any communication amongst ourselves impossible. The flight is thankfully going to be a short one, only about 45 minutes. Unbelievably, in a short while we are in the canyons of the Khumbu region. The clouds have lifted, and we are treated to the staggering beauty of the eastern Himalayan region. I have always had a great fascination with mountains and with the immovable nature and energy emitted from these formidable granite giants (the 'energy' a result of their cataclysmic beginnings). I have devoured many books on the subject: the successes and failures of those trying to scale the monster peaks. I have scrutinized with passion the innumerable and diverse maps and trails undertaken over the years on these heights, especially those known to be ambitious and immensely difficult: Everest, K2, the North face of the Eiger. Each one has stirred my imagination. As a lover of art, of inspiration and the expertise that follows, I have been awe-struck on many occasions, but two moments were absolute revelations. The hour I spent with the mural of Leonardo da Vinci's 'Last Supper' in Milan's Dominican convent, Santa Maria delle Grazie, will never fade from memory (the viewing, being the last of the evening, was extended past the usual 15 minutes). Even after restoration to remove added layers of paint, the splendor and dignity of the fresco was in no way diminished. The intimacy of being alone in the frigid cold air, sitting in front of the legendary North Face of the Eiger in the Swiss Bernese Alps, made for another extraordinary moment. While holding in gloved hands a cup of hot coffee, I perused and compared my maps detailing ascents dating from 1938, clearly seeing on the face the tortuous Death Bivouac, the Traverse of the Gods, the White Spider—a few of the most terrifying sections on the mountain. Immediately coming to mind are the early, fearless climbers such as Toni Kurz and Heinrich Harrer and the many others who took on the daunting task of climbing the ice and rock of the face. The Eiger, as Daniel Anker wrote: "Its very name inspires fear."[6]

I should not have thought about the word 'fear' and all that word evokes. In the cabin of this small aircraft, the excitement is not only palpable but has increased in intensity. The plane must be approaching Lukla. The scenery is beautiful; the plane is keeping parallel with the green mountains of the lower Himalayas, contrasting with the valleys beneath and even higher above, the mountains with snow reaching to the heavens. Coming into Lukla is an exact replica of the 'why did I read it' description. The plane has crossed a valley with the Dudh Kosi river visible far below with the runway coming immediately into view, at least I think it is a runway—a tiny, dirt track perched on the side of a mountain dead ahead. As I am sitting by a window, I can vouch for this airport being described as one of the most dangerous. It is surrounded by mountains—the "no go-around procedures" making complete sense. The pilots dip into the valley (OMG) then lifts at the last minute, landing onto the airstrip—a strip of dirt that is giving its best impression of being a runway. It is an extremely rough landing to say the least and just as hair-raising as imagined. Dead ahead was a 'wall'—in essence a mountain so high the top was not visible. Thankfully, the pilots make a quick right turn in avoidance —just in time.

---

6   Anker, Daniel, ed. *The Vertical Arena*, Mountaineers Books, 2000.

We live through the landing; everyone is clapping and cheering while I am breathing a sigh of relief. Tshering is expressionless, but then this is her home territory. One young man is holding his head in disbelief: "Oh my god," he bursts out. Unbelievably, we have arrived safely in Lukla, 9,300 feet above sea level. With rare clear skies above, Tshering and I step out of the plane. I retrieve the cello and, for the first time, take in what will be my environment for the next several months. Looking over the just-traversed valley, I wonder if a group of houses on a green mountain far in the distance is Sengma. A smell of juniper (perhaps from incense) joins the scent of spruce and fir from the encircling hills—all in all, beautiful surroundings. Standing for a moment next to my large cello case, I notice a few strange looks being sent in my direction. I would wager that the first time a cello has been seen on this runway is the here and now. I pull my jacket out of the pack, for it is chilly in the crisp mountain air, a pleasant change from the heat of Kathmandu. The majestic mountains behind the lower hills surrounding Lukla and looking north towards the Everest region are impossibly high and snow-covered. I know that those mountains, but even further north, loom as a threat to all those young, idealistic trekkers with whom I have just shared the journey from Kathmandu. A compact line of Sherpa guides and porters in charge of transporting equipment depart on a nearby path, the porters carrying more than their body weight in food and supplies. They are followed by those trekkers who are not only carrying their belongings but also their hopes in climbing what mountains lie ahead. A few cattle burdened with even more supplies, plod behind. Another group seems to be organizing themselves outside of the bustling airport office; this center also serving as the makeshift terminal.

Along with the loud roar of a plane warming up, there is activity on the runway. Evidently the rough landing (and no doubt an equally rough take-off) is because rocks help to make up the surface of the airstrip. A man and a boy (perhaps a father and son) are rushing out onto the dirt to carry away the larger stones that had flown onto the runway when our plane arrived. The explanation for our jolting landing becomes clear. I am assuming that they must work quickly before the next plane takes off or lands. Still recuperating from the experience of that landing, I look around at this place—at this little village with the smallest of airports in an area that has so much history. I will return to Lukla soon for email and finally, in three months, when I am on my way home. The airport, saddled with a truly terrible reputation, overshadows the importance and history of the town itself.

The name of this little village, 'Lukla,' means sheep corral, which is all it was before the airstrip was built in 1964. Now that I have arrived, I must say that I have the impression that little has happened to improve the runway since then. Lukla itself has certainly seen a great deal of growth since Sir Edmund Hillary supervised the construction of the landing strip as a starting point for treks toward Mount Everest Base Camp.[7] It remains so today. Quite a few young people are speaking excitedly to an officer evidently in charge of ticketing, waving their paper tickets in the air and wanting to be on the plane that is waiting, warming its engine, with cargo door open. Planes able to land and take off are necessarily small due to the short length of the runway; therefore, capacity on each plane is extremely limited. Those who have arrived in Lukla today are standing quietly together, patiently waiting for their expedition guides. There are no roads in Khumbu as can be readily seen as I look around—only paths spread out from the airport. All equipment for the high mountain climbs must be carried. The sole industry in this village is tourism, and with four to ten flights a day during the climbing season, everyone has their hands full.[8]

While Tshering looks for a sherpa to carry the cello, I decide to look around. The village itself looks neglected and a bit dilapidated with one story, stone and wood buildings surrounding the airport. It all looks a bit tired; nonetheless, the red tile rooftops give a splash of color to an otherwise drab atmosphere. On the

---

[7] *Tenzing-Hillary Airport*, https://en.wikipedia.org/wiki/Tenzing-Hillary_Airport
[8] McGuinness, *Trekking in the Everest Region*, 147-148.

other hand, the town is providing ground beneath my feet, and this is a welcome feeling. Putting the backpack on my shoulders and carrying the cello with its handle (the track wheels I had so carefully installed will no longer be helpful on this dirt), I decide to take this opportunity, using a small Lukla map that Tshering had provided, to investigate the communication situation in this village. During the coming months, I know that the desire to be in contact and to share my experiences with my family and friends will be of utmost importance. Since Pemba had assured me that email, phone, and postal services were available in Lukla (the town being a short distance from Sengma), this was my chance to locate my future source of communication with the outside world. Now I try to locate the 'X'—Tshering's mark for the location of the internet center. Patting myself on the back for seemingly going in the right direction, the map takes me on a dirt, incredibly uneven and stony path. As I pass by the Buddha Lodge and a few shops and other buildings in various stages of stone construction, several little boys, after checking out the lady with the big case, move past. They are dressed in identical red sweaters and caps with small backpacks on their shoulders, apparently walking from school. Finally, I discover a small, stone building with the sign, INTERNET CAFÉ. Unfortunately, the bright, blue trimmed door was locked; hopefully the person in charge is having lunch. A small piece of paper with writing in Nepali was tacked to the door frame; in my state of mind, the note must be predicting bad news. As I turn away, I unexpectedly bump into Tshering who has found a sherpa to carry the cello to Sengma. She sadly translates into English the paper on the entrance door: "closed indefinitely." *Great.* There is nothing I can do for the moment except wonder where the post office is located and assume there is a phone at the airport if I really needed to call someone. These questions will have to wait for another day, and I have no idea the practicality of making the return hike from Sengma.

With the actuality of no internet access, and with Tshering returning to Kathmandu tomorrow, I am worrying about being left alone—the consequence of desiring solitude. (I still cannot believe I thought a monk's cell was a good idea.) It is not as though I mind isolation. At times in my life I have searched for the opportunity to be alone. For a year after receiving my bachelor's degree, I rented a tiny, little cottage on farmland in Connecticut. Alone, save for numerous farm animals, the cottage was perfect for being able to practice and to have lessons with my teacher in an environment that was free of distraction. Peace and quiet was complete—an atmosphere not unlike the purpose and desire of this journey in Khumbu.

I had been optimistic that we would find someone to help with the cello. A young porter by the name of Diel, has been found at the Mera, the main trekker's lodge. Tshering quickly hired him to carry the cello. She and I backtrack to the lodge to find Diel, and with the cello on his back (finally the straps on the case are being put to good use), I tell the young man that he gives an impression of being a real cellist. Tshering translates; he smiles and then offers to carry the backpack as well. I am sure that such an instrument was unlike anything he has ever transported before. We are off in a northerly direction, joining the row of trekkers along a narrow, dirt path, soon leaving Lukla behind. Looking to the west, across the valley and lying across the face of a low mountain, Tshering points out the houses that make up the village of Sengma. I consider Pemba's remark that Sengma was a 'short distance' from Lukla. After we leave Chaurikharka, I daresay that the steep climb down the mountain will test my proclivity for precipitous descents. 2,000 feet below, at the bottom of the valley, a bridge crosses what looks to be a rather insignificant river; the climb up on the other side, unfortunately, looks to be an endurance test—one that will strain all belief in surviving the impossible. I try to put this concern elsewhere, at least for the time being.

Unfortunately, clouds are moving in from the south, and a light shower is beginning—I pull my rain gear out of the backpack. I ask Tshering about the end of the monsoon season and discover that for the rains to last through September would be unusual. I certainly do not want unusual; I want a standard monsoon timetable.

The path is now curving downhill, down some rocky steps and away from the main trekkers' path. The group of hikers and their companions continue their journey north. We are now quite alone. Diel and I follow Tshering down the rocky track leading to the village in which Tshering lived until moving to Kathmandu. Feeling as though I am not completely in control of all my faculties, I realize that I am just mentally tired. I am following along in a daze, seemingly waiting for the next hurdle. The narrow trail is packed dirt but filled with uneven rocks, causing me to watch every step I take in order to prevent an accident. This being my first hike since leaving Colorado, I am pleasantly surprised that I am not having much difficulty, even at this altitude of almost 10,000 feet. With Tshering leading the way, we are up one hill and down the next, scrub trees of pine and fir lining the pathway, and ever-present stone steps gradually leading us downwards. I have the distinct feeling that I have left forever a horizontal path—never to be trod again. Passing a small field of yellow mustard flowers, the sweet smell of the plant fills the air (I had no idea the plant smells like clover or vanilla). We move aside for a man passing slowly by; his cargo looms out four feet across and towers above his head, all attached to his back with a strap across his forehead. I trust that his destination is not miles away. That question will remain unanswered, for we have arrived at a sign directing us straight ahead to Chaurikharka. The man turns right, his footsteps so measured that they make no sound.

Joined by the occasional dog and cat—the dogs happily welcoming us to town, the cats more wary--we walk along the sloping, rocky footpaths leading into the village. The trail is slippery, dampened from the brief rain shower. Terraces are built into the land behind a small group of one-story, stucco houses on our left; and, on our right, a canopy of vegetation over a high wall is a prediction of flowers in the coming months. Elements of the Buddhist culture, that which will permeate my life in the days ahead, come into sight as we progress onward. A great number of *mani* stones inscribed with religious prayers (*mantras*) are lining the path in rows of considerable length and height— some imposing and much taller than I, and some smaller, flat inscribed stones. The trail becomes much smoother; flat stones in mortar are winding along as we come into the village. We begin to pass typical Sherpa homes, most appearing to be made of stone, stuccoed with cement; their window and door frames painted in a vibrant blue or green. Outdoor lines hold washing, probably still wet as the rain must have been unexpected. We come to a fairly large, walled *stupa* (monument) with a gold steeple, lined with Buddhist flags and with rows of *mani* stones inscribed with the prayer, "*Om mani padme hum.*" Prayer wheels are set into niches along the wall. The structure is reminiscent in appearance to the Boudhanath *stupa* in Kathmandu, although much, much smaller. The cylindrical wheels are turned as we pass—always clockwise. Tshering tells me that turning the wheels instills one with the same effect as orally reciting the prayers inscribed on the outside of each cylinder.

After a few minutes of meandering along curving paths, we arrive at Tshering's house, a home fronted by a loosely arranged stone wall, the wall covered completely with yellow rhododendrons. I step for the first time into a typical Sherpa home, a household built and arranged in the Sherpa Buddhist tradition. Meeting Tshering's mother and stepfather, I give voice to the two syllables I know in Sherpa, "*Tong boo*," (hello). Her mother is wearing the long skirt and colorful apron of a Sherpa woman; and with her lively personality, reminds me of Tshering. Full of smiles, I can tell by mother and daughter's cheerful chatter that they are overjoyed to see each other. Looking around, I am in the middle of a large living space, shelves with containers encompassing an entire wall, the containers no doubt for food and storage. There are rows of beautiful brass dishes, an altar, benches for sitting and probably sleeping (no beds are obvious), and an open hearth—a large black pot sits on a grate above carefully laid wood. As the fireplace grate is away from the wall, its placement causes me to wonder what happens to the smoke. Tshering is translating much of what is being communicated—why I am about to devote a few months across the valley playing the cello. Her parents, after looking at the large case, nod and smile appreciatively. I doubt that they truly understand although it would be wonderful if they did realize the nature of my venture. Moments of recognition for my undertaking, and perhaps even a small amount of validation, have been few and far between since arrival in Nepal. On the other hand, why should they understand, and why is it seemingly important to me right now?

Tshering's mother offers me a wonderful cup of spicy, black tea; and afterward, I take a magical photo of Tshering, her mother and stepfather standing happily in front of the shelves. Excusing myself, I then encounter my first experience with the quintessential Sherpa outhouse: a small lean-to built on the side of the house. I was expecting the structure's rough and simple configuration as Pemba had mentioned that there is little plumbing in the region—none, in Sengma. Hope that plumbing had arrived at Chaurikharka and Sengma without Pemba's knowledge died quickly.

After a goodbye, *"khole zhue,"* Tshering, Diel and I walk along another dirt track, this one leaving the village as we begin the drop into the valley. The descent is an incredibly steep, seemingly vertical path as we move slowly toward the Dudh Kosi. I am calling it a 'path,' but our legs are brushing against short fir trees and shrubs as we move steadily down. Only Tshering seems to know where to plant her feet. Naturally she is leading the way; and although I absolutely recognize that she and Diel could run down this mountain, she is being very mindful of my pace. Glancing behind me, I see that Diel is now carrying the cello case on his shoulders, evidently feeling that this is the more comfortable position. For the first time in my life, I am worrying more about my safety than that of the cello. This instrument has been my partner for almost thirty years; it will not forsake me right now.

An hour later, we are continuing our slow descent. We are taking a longer detour down to the bridge due to an avalanche of a few days before, the result cutting us off from the shorter route. The landslide was caused by the constant rain of the past months—the continuing monsoon weather. As we descend further, the roar of the torrent of water that is the Dudh Kosi becomes augmented with every step we take (my past description of 'insignificant' must have been the perspective of height and distance). Finally, we come to the bridge that will take us over to the other side. Tshering wants me to cross first (why, I am not sure, unless it is the Buddhist way, or I am a test subject). I negotiate very carefully what seems to be a make-shift bridge of planks that bounce with every step I take, and with ropes for handrails all is not steady; in fact, there are points where I can see the river rushing below through spaces between the individual boards. Once across, I turn around and absolutely have a duty to take another photo. It will be one for the books with Tshering leading Diel and the cello—the water below. Realizing that I have indeed survived the hike down, I take a moment to think about what the instrument is going through, hoping that Diel realized the importance of what he is carrying (I do not think so, but one can hope). Thinking of the cello, I am thankful that I turned the prayer wheels of Chaurikharka more than once. Tshering, as we look at the view down below, tells me that this river is known as the 'Relentless River of Everest.' It is the main waterway that rushes down from Everest and the high mountains. Now I look upwards—another 2,000 feet skyward to Sengma.

The path uphill is similar to the previous struggle down (shrubs lining the nonexistent trail), with only Tshering knowing the true way. The hike upwards is relentless; the sound of the river diminishing from a resounding reverberation to a minor rumbling. We make an abrupt stop at one point—a leech is attached to my leg. After I make a small commotion, Tshering, the recipient of my undying thanks, removes the small animal. Yes, it is an invertebrate ANIMAL, and one I have never brushed up against in the Rockies. I am an absolute coward when it comes to small beings. After that fright we keep moving, eventually climbing the last few feet and rounding the top of the hill. Sengma is straight ahead. It is difficult to call Sengma a village as it is simply a group of houses on the side of a mountain. I walk the steep, upward muddy path with Tshering and Diel, my breathing finally giving me difficulty as I tread ever higher. The vista surrounding me is not unlike the hill just climbed—green shrubs and the occasional expanse of yellow flowers as far as I can see. There are low-lying clouds drifting in front of us; even so, I can see the tops of even higher mountains behind the ridge. The homes, seemingly clinging to the side of the mountain, are situated separately—some distance apart. All are built with the same, basic Sherpa structure: two story buildings of stone with a ridge roof, the lower floor built into the hill behind it. After passing four or five houses, we arrive at Chongba's home, the house in which I will spend the next three months. Tshering shows me the location of the outhouse, after which we enter the ground floor (this floor is for the cattle and farm tools) and climb the wooden stairs to the second; this upper floor being the family's living space. I immediately smell the remnants of juniper incense; some other odor is unidentifiable.

The first order of business is to meet Chongba's wife (and Tshering's sister), Phuti, and their two girls, Mingma Phuti (ten) and Pasang Lhmu (five). In the same fashion as Tshering's mother, Phuti is dressed in Sherpa style with a long woolen skirt and a striped, multicolored apron—all in wild contrast to Tshering's western clothing. Phuti is an elegantly tall woman with a solemn, almost austere demeanor that I find surprising contrasted with the quick and easy laughter of her sister. The two little girls are beautiful; they are smiling and happy to see Tshering and probably wondering about me and that unfathomably large white object. Chongba will not be home for quite a while; he is leading a trek in the Annapurna mountains. Diel announces that he must leave us and return to Lukla; I assume he will run home in record time. Phuti offers a yak butter tea (that was the smell—like a salty cheese). After a mouthful of what had the texture of a light soup, I decided that the end of my yak butter tea experience had arrived. Hoping no one is noticing, I put the cup down and put all my concentration into the attempt to understand, through the grandiose gesturing, what is being said. The second order of business: to view my new surroundings. The family has been thoughtful enough to create a small room for me with a real bed off to the side of the main living area—a room with enough space to practice. As I look around, I am understanding the entire picture: the family must sleep on either the benches that are organized against the wall, or on the floor itself. I feel badly as I am paying them so little for 'board and room' for the next few months, and I have the only comfortable sleeping arrangement. Of course, I realize that people, to rest or sleep, do not need something soft to lie on; in fact, a 'bed' used to be a pile of straw. I still feel guilty. The third order of business begins right away and is giving the impression of becoming the most brilliant—a welcome party. Sharing a bottle of whisky that Tshering brought from Kathmandu, I am thankful that the drink has wiped out all remembrance of the yak butter tea. The warm, intense liquid along with a dish of steamed rice is welcome after a day of anxious travel.

By now it is early evening, and quite dark outside; the only light in the house is emanating from a few candles placed on the sides of the iron stove, a reminder that there is no electricity in Sengma. I am so very tired, but evidently there is one more place to go. An uncle and a small child had been caught up in the recent avalanche, in the very ravine that we had crossed just a short while ago. A Buddhist death ritual is taking place in the house at the top of the hill. Lamas from a neighboring village have arrived, and we are going to attend. I had only been in Sengma for an hour or two; and now, grabbing my flashlight from the backpack, we are hiking to another house in this little settlement for a funeral. There is a matter-of-fact way in which everyone is acting that is surprising to me, even though I realize that for the Buddhist the funeral does not mean the end, it is a beginning. For this reason, the service is not necessarily a sad affair. For my part, I am caught up in the thought of the two relatives losing their lives, and in that valley. I am about to experience a Buddhist funeral as part of the introduction to this little community. I cannot think of anything more startling. This time I bring up the rear as we walk upward. Beyond mentally and physically tired, I have an irresistible need to sleep; to recover from the day and to possess a chance at a new start tomorrow.

As we arrive at the house, I see that the structure is typically Sherpa, just longer horizontally—perhaps two houses undivided. On the second floor, monks of all ages and in red robes are sitting on benches along one side of the large living space. Another, older in demeanor and standing in front of an altar, is reciting what must be the Tibetan Book of the Dead. It is one thing to read about a Buddhist funeral; being suddenly immersed in this religious tradition—the rebirth of the spirit, is absolutely another. Other women from the village had arrived, joining the monks in prayer. About 20 people are in the room, including the holy men, Tshering, Phuti and me. Before we left the house, I had been given a bowl of rice to bring to the ritual. Following the others, I placed a handful on the altar, the shrine itself covered with small statues, photos, *chakra* (healing) stones and flags. In the dimly lit room (candles are glowing) and feeling a bit lost, I find a seat next to Tshering, someone who is bringing a sense of familiarity to the moment. I smell a new, unfamiliar incense filling the area—I am guessing a mixture of musk and amber, known to be commonplace to this traditional service. The room is hushed and still, other than the constant drone of the monk. I have read a bit about this service, even reading a translated version of the Book of the Dead. This is the moment when the transition begins for the deceased's rebirth. The Book is being read to guide the soul through the transformation— the rice being presented as an offering of grain, as the soul is nearby. This transition for the dead could last up to 49 days, prayers given every seven days to help the dead pass into the next life. It is hard to believe that I am in the middle of a ritual as an outsider and yet have been brought into this community of Sherpas without question. I look around at the faces—worn and weary, a legacy of farming and herding left to them by the Sherpas of the 16th century, traders that migrated down to the Khumbu region from Tibet.[9] I am surrounded by history.

---

9   Ibid., 105-106

The reading has ceased, and my exhausted mind is trying to fathom what is happening. The monks sitting on the opposite bench are now making their own music on a wide assembly of instruments. I have heard Tibetan music previously, but not eight feet away and in such a serious environment. It is extraordinary—the sound of these instruments haunting and, in a sense, unearthly. The percussion instruments, the drums, cymbals and bells are handheld—the wind instruments include a *ghyaling* (played and sounding like a double reed oboe-like instrument) and the long *tonquin* horns (two meters long, although as they can telescope, in a larger space, they could be much longer). The horns produce an eerie, mournful resonance—unlike anything, live, I have heard before.

We take our leave when the musicians end their part of the ritual. As we walk back to the house, in a moment of complete simplification, I think about wanting to end my journey before it even began. Death does not mean the end but a beginning—an analogy of sorts. I know that I will be seeing the holy men again as they will be remaining in Sengma for the 49 days of prayer. And it is true: in the following weeks I often saw the monks standing on the hillside, dressed in their red robes, taking a break from the ceremony. I am not sure when they left the area.

It was hard to believe this first day—beginning in Kathmandu and ending in Sengma. The flight, the crushingly, relentlessly long hike, the death service with the music; it was unbelievable, but I made it. Tshering is leaving in the morning, so she takes the opportunity to discuss with Phuti what to expect in the next few months: the possibility of taking me to see Everest, the project with the cello (I pulled the cello out of the case for explanatory reasons), the projected schedule for my leaving Sengma—the overall course of action. After seeing the cello, Tshering feels that the house could become too cold for the wood of the instrument by the end of November; that moving down to an area closer to Kathmandu might be for the best. She and Dinesh have some friends in a terraced, hill-top village, Nagarkot, that may have room in their hotel. With all plans sorted out and with a last swallow of whisky, the first evening in Sengma ends. Saying good night, *"khole zim,"* I take possession of a candle and make a move to my small, but so appreciated room.

After all the preparation, I have finally arrived at my home for the next few months. I am drained and worn out but gratified to be settled; and after today, dare I say it —alive. The question of existing will, I have a feeling, remain with me every day. Outside my window there is fog overlaying the pitch-blackness; the rain will begin again soon. When I am less tired and on a cloudless night, I wonder what the stars will look like on a mountain with no lights in any direction. I tumble into my sleeping bag (still feeling guilty about sleeping on the only bed) and fall asleep with the sound of rain falling, only gradually realizing that it is the sound of the Dudh Kosi coursing through the valley. I know monsoon weather has not ended and will provide dampness and gloom; but tomorrow, no matter the weather, I begin. Bach awaits.

When I awake, the house is quiet. I dress quickly as there is a slight chill (I will no doubt be living in my long underwear). Going past glowing wood in the fireplace, I go downstairs to find the outhouse. I woke up during the early hours, but my surroundings were dark and a trifle foreboding. The stairs will be a real hurdle at night. Making my way to the outdoor toilet in the unlit house, through the sleeping family, down the stairs and past the (perhaps) not-so-sleeping cattle, will be daunting even with my trusty flashlight. It will be less problematic not to bother with this nighttime interruption unless a true emergency.

This is the moment to investigate outside; as I remember, the outhouse is conveniently close. The usual morning ablutions, washing and brushing teeth, will have to be postponed as the description of where to locate water was completely lost to me last night. Luckily there are no cattle on the first floor; I am not prepared for that actuality. A classic outhouse is to the right. The shed is representative of all outdoor toilets known to man but perhaps a little less private than most—exposure from the front is absolute. No one is thankfully around.

Before returning upstairs, I hear Tshering and Phuti on the lower path. Tshering is about to leave Sengma. She will be staying in Chaurikharka, leaving for Kathmandu in a couple of days. Tshering gives last instructions and answers my final questions (about hiking, the weather, the animals downstairs, and the water). I am thankful for all of this before the language barrier sets in. She explains that hiking would be fine but that I should not climb the higher hills behind the house; a tiger has just attacked cattle. I had read that Bengal tigers are in Khumbu, but it is disheartening to hear that they are near civilization. *Great.* Her advice is always given very matter-of-factly—clearly, it seems to me, out of proportion to the real danger. Her desire to share causes more trepidation if that is even possible. Of other wild animals in the vicinity, she mentions that there are macaque monkeys on the paths leading to Ghat, the village further north—the same species of monkeys that inhabit the Monkey Temple in Kathmandu. I am ecstatic to hear that Phuti has agreed to guide me on a trek to see Everest sometime in October; and in late November, if necessary because of the cold, Tshering will arrive to give assistance in returning to the Kathmandu area. Sadly, I see Tshering walk back down the path to begin the climb to Lukla. I say to myself, "there goes my last communication in English for the near future." This turns out to be only partially true.

After boiling water on the fire, Phuti makes me a cup of very strong black tea. Together we share a silent moment as she busies herself in the kitchen area. She is very, very serious, a truly no-nonsense woman. After saying a few words in Sherpa, unquestionably letting me know what she is intending to do, she heads downstairs. I must figure out how to say, "Where are you going? Can I help?" It would be comforting to be involved. For now, with Tshering gone, I am, for all intents and purposes, alone.

Sighing, I return to explorations. My learning curve about Sherpa living continues to reach new heights, but there is much more to learn and understand. Retracing my steps downstairs to the ground floor, I see some roughly hewn garden tools, a stockpile of wood for the fire and enclosures for the cattle. Evidently the cattle are in the higher hills; they will be brought down to the house in the winter. These stalls are far removed from the wooden stairs leading upward—undeniably less anxiety for me. I heard the term 'yuk-yaks' for the first-time last night. This is Phuti's name for their cattle: hybrids of cows and yaks, the domesticated yak being found further north. These hybrids constitute the working cattle in Khumbu, carrying goods and equipment on the farmland and on treks.

As I experienced last night, the upper floor is the place where everything happens. I have learned that all houses in a Sherpa village are built with the windows facing in the same direction, assuming the landscape is accommodating—in Sengma, east. In this manner, the home is exposed to the warmth of the sun. There are no doors or windows in the back of the house for the opposite reason; architecturally because most houses are built into a hillside (hence the steep walk from house to house in Sengma). In this small village, all homes are arranged in the same manner and for the same objectives.

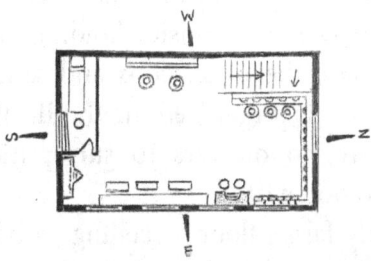

The water system is a simple hose, the water coming from higher altitudes on the mountain—the hose emptying into a large pot in the kitchen area. Wisdom dictates that there are indeed animals up in the hills from whence the water begins its journey to the individual homes (the tigers come into mind). Accordingly, I commit to boiling (and, under the circumstances, quite possibly purifying) all water that I am intending to drink. I collect some water into a basin found on a nearby shelf, solving the immediate dilemma of washing. Now, what to do with the used water in the basin. I am trying the 'out the window' method (the most unobtrusive window being in my room), first checking to see if no one (animal or human) is below. Brushing my teeth will have to wait until I can come to grips with the purification gadget. I am definitely making this up as I go along.

The iron fireplace, open on the front with a grate for cooking, is on the wall with the windows. When Phuti boiled the tea, the smoke escaped through an opening in the wooden slats of the roof. I had heard tales of yak dung being used for burning, but evidently dung is only used higher in the Khumbu region, above the tree line where little wood is available. Questions are gradually being answered. If I do not want to always bathe with cold water, I must become expert in starting a fire; on second thought, perhaps cold water will do. One small step at a time.

Low wooden tables are in front of the long benches. Despite the benches, I believe that the family sleeps on the floor (unwarranted guilt again). On the window-less wall, pots of all sizes sit on the shelves—the taller pots, directly on the floor. These pots Tshering had intimated, will soon be storing vegetables to be consumed in the winter. More shelves are opposite, holding incredibly beautiful brass plates alongside the usual cups and saucers. Every single object in this space is organized methodically in the Sherpa tradition. There are no drawers to surreptitiously investigate; indeed, drawers do not exist.

An impressively large, floor to ceiling wooden altar (*gompa*) faces my room. In every Buddhist home, this is the place for prayers in the morning to protect the house; and indeed, when I awoke, I smelled the sharp aroma of juniper. Buddhism is no longer peripheral at this point; it is the center. My past interest in Buddhism has been superficial; however, this interest has always nagged at the corners of thought, unrelenting in its mission to make itself more essential in my life. It has, as can be seen, been instrumental in bringing me to Sengma. Years ago, I had read about the courageous monks in the caves, devoting themselves to their teachings. I then began an examination of Buddhist philosophy with readings such as the Dalai Lama's *Freedom in Exile*[10] and Robert Thurman's *The Tibetan Book of the Dead*.[11] These books, and others like them, led me to a curiosity about Tibetan Buddhism—Tibetan in preference to the other established Buddhist traditions.

It has been an unlikely marriage of thought for as a child I was Episcopalian. My father, coming from Sussex in the UK and from the Church of England, knew the close relationship between the Episcopal and Anglican churches. He always had a common-sense attitude toward dying, that it is at the end of life for all—no worries. The years spent on this earth, in the Buddhist tradition, were simply preparation for death. He would have been a wonderful Buddhist for he always lived his life knowing this precept. My mother and father, both musicians and wonderful parents, prepared well and made the most of their years in living.

Grabbing my topological map of the region, I step outside once more with a relatively clear head following the intensely strong tea. My intention is to take a short hike along the pathway between the houses and further up the hill. The weather seems promising: drifting clouds below a blue sky. The scenery is magnetic and magnificent—the snow-topped mountains ringing the valley are ever-present. Mindful of the tigers, I will forgo a long hike up the mountain. Like a proverbial cat who makes ever larger circles around its home until sure of its surroundings, I decide to stay in the area. This time, I will be seeing what was missed last evening in the dark. I don't see Phuti or others from the village; perhaps they are working in the fields surrounding the houses. Mingma and Pasang are now in the dusty yard playing seesaw, sitting on either end of a rough, wooden board loosely propped over a stone wall in front of the house. The board looks slightly precarious, but I am a believer in children learning to be mindful about their own safety; that being said, I have no idea how to say, "be careful!" Moreover, they are smiling and happy. I

---

10   Dalai LamaXIV, *Freedom in Exile: The Autobiography of the Dalai Lama*, Harper Collins, 1990.

11   Thurman, Robert, *The Tibetan Book of the Dead*, Penguin Random Books, 1993.

smile and say, "*tong boo;*" they provide me with a questioning glance as I move on. (I decide to figure out how to be friends as soon as possible.) Walking a slight distance on a rocky, muddy path toward the larger 'funeral' house, I see two monks in their red robes standing on a huge boulder to the right, to all appearances having an interlude in their prayers. No longer hiking upwards in the pitch-dark as I had done last night, I see a stream amongst the rocky ground, running down from a waterfall above. A large *mani* stone with an upright white flag sits alongside a bridge of wooden logs crossing the stream; and it is here I see Phuti and several other women in the water, scrubbing clothes against the rocks. I wave to say good morning. They take a quick look but continue with their laundry. Watching the women work, to me there is no doubt that this is a difficult life.

Returning to the house and finding a spot to sit on the low, stone wall, I take a moment to look around, to smell the roses so to speak. Not roses but stunning yellow flowers swarm against the loosely constructed rock walls. I breathe in deeply. I think of Phuti doing her laundry against the rocks. When faced with a difficulty causing me dissatisfaction, I try to find a solution—how to halt my 'suffering' from the very start. I may even try to discontinue the action. In so doing, I would be taking an easy path, for that would be the time to learn and to prepare. For the Buddhist, following the Noble Eightfold Path, the right view, resolve, speech, action, livelihood, effort, mindfulness, and concentration, allows an individual to reach an enlightened state when dissatisfaction has ceased. I am ashamed of my over-simplification, but it is my general truth. There is so much to learn.[12]

The breeze, crisp and invigorating, is not unlike the Rockies. I gaze to the east and north catching sight of majestically high, snow-covered mountains surrounding this valley. My map tells me that to the east, across the Dudh Kosi, lie the peaks of Gonglha at almost 20,000 feet and Kusum Kangguru, even taller at almost 21,000 feet.

---

12 Holmes, David Dale, *Understanding the Four Noble Truths and the Noble Eightfold Path*, Buddhistdoor Global, https://www.buddhistdoor.net/features/understanding-the-four-noble-truths-and-walking-the-noble-eightfold-path/ July 19, 2021

Although very much in the distance Kangguru still towers from afar, a waterfall cascading from the snow-covered heights. Having had an interest in meditation, I wonder if this waterfall could become a focal point, not only in terms of concentration and in bringing a sense of calm into what I fear will be a natural state of distress, but also in my practicing. It might be interesting to see if I could meditate while attempting to memorize these suites.

Further to the north, following the river and the path across the way to Everest, the snowy crests of the high Himalayas can clearly be seen in the far distance. On this western side of the Dudh Kosi, the view is unhindered. This land that surrounds me could convince anyone that Nepal is, indeed, the highest country in the world. I must enjoy these unobstructed views while I am able—in between the recurring rains of the monsoon.

Even surrounded from on high with snow and ice, Sengma is primarily farmland although with few flowers, the space around me apparently reserved for growing vegetables and wheat. The flowers I can recognize appear to be yellow rhododendrons (similar to those on the wall by the house) or varied violet-colored primrose. I can barely make out the trekkers on the path across the river as they appear to be a slow-moving caravan of ants (I am credulous that, in my packing, I did not visualize the need for binoculars). Despite the distance, I can still catch a glimpse of the sherpa guides and the porters with extraordinary amounts of objects on their backs, the loads ready to be handed off to trekkers upon arrival at the base camps. In the future, how wonderful it would be to spend time with those traveling further north—to ask questions about their objectives and lives. One day I will cross the river again.

That last comment seems sad. Distress, another form of sadness, unfortunately takes over from time to time—visually in the form of dark clouds moving up the river from the south. The trekkers and climbers heading north must certainly hope that the tail-end of the monsoon weather is upon us. For myself, if the monsoon season remains with us considerably longer, I will find it a huge challenge to find comfort in a cold, dark stone house—it is unlike any home

I have ever experienced. Although I am at the beginning of this journey, I have already met enough challenges for the time being.

During our years together, my quartet faced many challenges as we travelled all over the world. Our two tours to the capitals of the former Soviet Union are prime examples. After a series of concerts in Moscow and Leningrad in the fall of 1985, we became the first American classical ensemble to give a full tour of the country. Having no cultural exchange agreement between our two countries as we crossed that vast expanse made the travel precarious. There were times that I was uneasy and anxious and perhaps even a bit frightened (for example, at the prospect that our conversation at the dinner table was being monitored). Nevertheless, the four of us solved the problems that arose. Finding solutions to the challenges that one faces is so much easier when you have companionship. Depending only upon yourself can be intimidating, at best.

The timidity that I felt as a young person has always been difficult to overcome; but in one area, performing for others always gave me stability and courage. Walking out on stage to perform, although not putting oneself in physical harm, is an internal challenge. It is a test to see if the music can move, can stir the emotions of the listener; and, even after many concerts a year for the past fifty years, each performance has had its own reward. In other things, I have always tried to assume an air of confidence—one that often belies the true nature of my feelings. And, if I am being truthful, I must admit that I love the **idea** of a challenge. Once I put my mind to the fact that an idea is possible, 'full steam ahead' is the only speed I consider. I once drove alone down the east coast of Italy from Bonefro (in the region of Molise) to Bari, Lecce, and Santa Maria di Leuca in Puglia, the latter city on the coast at the southernmost tip of the boot. The plan was then to swing north to Matera (a magical city in Basilicata), returning to Bonefro. My Italian friends said, "Aren't you afraid to go by yourself?" Perhaps I was, but the delight of thinking about being a tourist with no obligations to anyone else, overcame any thoughts of worry.

All had gone smoothly until I departed from Santa Maria. Unfortunately, shortly after I left the coast, I was followed down a main motorway by a mystery fellow in a green car. Becoming nervous, I decided that perhaps I was being a bit paranoid, and that he was harmlessly just heading in the same direction. Wanting to verify that thought, I quickly turned off at an exit. When he followed me into the piazza of a very small town (not a person was in sight), I had to admit that this situation was not good. I made a quick U-turn into a narrow, one-way street. I saw a young man sitting on a motorcycle talking to an elderly couple on a stoop. I stopped; and, probably looking frightened, he asked if I needed help. I told him that I was being followed by a green car. He asked, "What green car?" I turned to point at the end of the street; and, at that very moment, the green car turned in, stopped, and, after 30 seconds, backed out. A film was in the making, at least in my mind. The happy ending: the young man hopped on his bike and led me back to the highway, keeping watch for the car. At that point a 'man' was not following me—the stalker was instead, **a green car** (Stephen King's novel, 'Christine,' comes to mind). According to an Italian friend, it was all just a test! All in all, I am going to say that little successes build character; this challenge, bizarrely, served me well in later years.

Not unlike meeting the challenges of the past, I will summon all the confidence and courage available to me in the next few months. Interrupting my memories, I smell a pungent aroma of frying onions and spices: lunch. Phuti has returned and has prepared *dal bhat*—lentils and rice. I snag my dictionary from my room and sit down with Phuti on leather stools in front of the fireplace, the girls sitting on the bench. I am ravenous as I have not eaten since last night—the bill of fare being steamed white rice, a granola bar from my backpack, and whisky. The *dal bhat* is deliciously spicy and made with red lentils, the taste being quite unusual for this typical Nepali dish (except for the curry, the spices are difficult to recognize). I sought information from my 'book' and attempted a couple of phrases: "Food is good," "You have a good morning?" Phuti answered, but I have not the foggiest idea what she said nor the meaning of the accompanying gesture. My number one difficulty in learning a new language: I can become versed in a question but in the speed of the response, I am lost in the detail. "Thank you" (*thuche*) is understood and received with a smile, and I retreat to my room.

The cello stands at the ready—no doubt confused that for almost a week, I have not played a note. I bring out my Alexanian score of the suites—the identical volume I studied as a student thirty years prior. As I am, hopefully, going to be drawing new conclusions and insights into these works of Bach, not as a twenty-year-old student but as a traveler of life, perhaps a new score of my own design is in the future! Written into this familiar score is a strategy—a detailed master plan of how to proceed that I had organized before leaving for Nepal, the division of sections within each dance movement being the primary strategy. It is a way to begin although I believe in flexibility—with changing a strategy when necessary. Sitting on a stool that I have swiped from alongside the fireplace, my orientation is to the east and through the front windows. Facing east is the direction the sun will rise—this orientation being the source of inspiration and light. What a perfect alignment of location and purpose. The perspective from my little room is impossible to describe adequately: out the window I can see the inconceivably high Kusum Kangguru and the eastern mountains. From this vantage point I can also clearly see the waterfall falling from the height of the mountain—my meditation inspiration. Sitting for a moment with this majestic view across the valley, I ponder the months ahead.

Since I arrived in Kathmandu and now, Sengma, I have felt scared and alone in this uncustomary environment, completely at odds with the purpose of my trip. I doubt that I thought through this Nepali challenge except for the fundamentals and the irresistible urge of adventure. The over-arching worry: I wonder if I am equipped to handle what lies ahead. The big fear— safety. I contemplate the possibility of becoming ill from the food, falling off a cliff, having a heart attack at this altitude, or being attacked by the unknown animal life, specifically the tiger that I know will enter my thoughts if I exceed my boundaries. Normally, I would not have unintelligent thoughts such as these; but despite it all, I believe that the lack of communication with the inside and outside world (the latter, a first for me) is also affecting my sense of security. I will try email or snail mail sooner or later; but for that to transpire, Tshering has described quite a circuitous route. Someone will arrive at Sengma, collect my letter or written email, run the message to Lukla ('run' is the impressive word here) put the mail on a plane to Kathmandu, give the message to Dinesh at his service, and finally—for Dinesh to forward to the States. For me to receive a piece of mail basically means the reverse action must take place. I understand that all I need is time—time to adjust to these new conditions. It is not exaggeration, however, when I say that survival is paramount on my mind. Even so, I am confident that I will make sense of it all. There is just a tremendous amount to learn.

Putting thoughts aside, I remove the cello from its case, and suddenly all seems right and beautifully familiar. Having played the cello for 50 years, it is an old friend. Holding the instrument in my hands, I am hopeful that all will be tolerable for it, and for me. Unbelievably the instrument is still in tune, and no strings have broken since my hotel room at The Nirvana, even after the conditions it was put under in the past couple of days (Diel, thank you so much). My overall plan is to begin, naturally, with the first suite—the Suite in G Major, proceeding on with each successive suite in order. This G Major suite, the opening work in the entire opus and the suite most often performed, is so light-hearted and cheerful in nature that I know I will smile through every note. I am eager to get the project underway—to begin the discovery, for spending these three months with the beauty of Bach, for the actual daily routine, will give me the calm and unworried atmosphere I need to sustain myself.

There are six dance movements that make up each suite: Prelude, Allemande, Courante, Sarabande, Minuet (or Bourree or Gavotte) and Gigue. One could ask if the movements have a specific 'place' in the composition; for example, the Sarabande may contemplate the mood of the entire suite, the Gigue may synthesize the whole—all to be considered but perhaps better left to the listener. Within the six suites, there are 36 movements in total. I will not wait to begin the sixth suite; for me, this one is the most difficult, and the suite that I never studied as a student. My plan, while practicing each suite in turn, is to work on a portion of the sixth suite every day until time to devote to it my full attention.

With the overall study, I have made a rather complicated schedule—one that typifies how I work, especially with memorization. The schedule, I admit, is excessively fastidious as I have placed small and large divisions of each movement into the schedule in a certain order. If I am to complete the project in these few months, for me this is the 'way' and it will be successful. I must also add that I have used this approach to memorization with other mediums such as poems and written literary works. My schedule for Bach in Nepal goes like this:

Day 1:
- Read through Suite 1 in its entirety (all six movements), with the music.
- Prelude (the first movement), read through again, with the music.
- Memorize Section A of the Prelude.
- Work on Sections B-F.
- Perform Section A, without the music.
- Work on Suite VI.

Day 2:
- Read through Suite 1 in its entirety, with the music.
- Prelude, read through again, with the music.
- Memorize Section B of the Prelude.
- Work on Sections C-F.
- Perform Sections A and B, without the music.
- Work on Suite VI.

Above all, my underlying motto is that 'a good plan is a flexible plan.' I will have no problem changing the entire schedule if necessary.

By 'study' I intend to question everything: new bowings, new fingerings, new phrases—all may be warranted. Every single aspect of the music will be considered. Old routine habits will perhaps be discarded or put on the Socratic shelf of memory. I realize that this could sound as if I have embraced the idea of a substantial, unpleasant undertaking; however, I believe that one can find and reach, in the Buddhist tradition, a point of bliss and joy in practice.

The first Bach Suite is the one most widely played, probably due to its cheerful nature—its uncomplicated way of saying, 'life should be as effortless as possible.' I have been travelling for a week. Now I am ready to begin the discovery. I will bring the accumulation of the experiences I have had in my professional life, not only to new discoveries in Bach but to those that can inform the rest of my life.

I launch into the Prelude of the first suite—the familiarity of my rocking arm producing the opening arpeggios bringing a smile to my lips. Through the open windows, the sound of the arpeggios resounds in the mountains. As I am playing, I make the decision to begin my practice with this Prelude every single day. In so doing, due to the Prelude's inherent optimism, the sun will metaphorically be emerging; and as I will always be facing east due to the limitation of space in my little room, the newness of the day will stimulate further inspiration. The sound in this room, surrounded by wood, is warm and resounding—acoustically perfect (acousticians have yet to learn that a wooden shoebox configuration for a concert hall creates the optimum resonance!). The key of G Major generates the lyrical, rather regal nature of this suite; the phrases are comforting, rustic, gentle and peaceful. There is also an improvisatory, joyful nature to the music—a feeling that I hope will extend into my life at Sengma. It is perfect for the beginning.

SUITE I

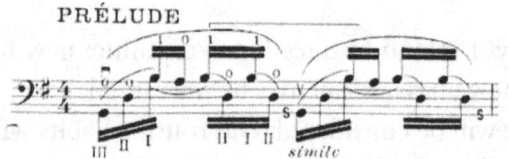

Having wondered if this Sherpa family will appreciate Bach, the sound of the cello for the first time attracts to my room a small audience of two—Mingma and Pasang. They listened for approximately two minutes before playing outside seemed a better alternative. Their curiosity had been satisfied. I suppose the reaction is a comment on Casals' musing—that Bach could be understood by everyone. Perhaps it is all too new for Mingma and Pasang; that it will take a bit of time for Bach to grow on them. For now, for myself, the G Major Prelude is enough.

The first few days in Sengma move past in a daze. I settle into the morning tea and toast (the latter browned in a frying pan) and the daily lunch of rice, vegetable *dal* and boiled potatoes (the latter also in pancake form), all with an ample amount of black tea. Phuti seems to have developed an exceedingly spicy chili sauce of mashed chilis, garlic and onion (if I could drink the water out of the hose, a gallon would not have been enough to soothe the taste buds). The sauce is a staple in the *dal* and, in general, every vegetable dish. Phuti's potatoes pancakes are grated on a homemade contraption: a piece of metal with holes formed by a nail and fastened onto a small wooden board. After adding flour, the mixture is shaped on a curved plate, then cooked; it is insanely good, not to mention, creatively produced.

At meals, for the most part, I take a place on one of the benches and sit quietly as Mingma and Pasang chatter away. I sit quietly except for the few words that speak of the weather: 'sun' (*nyima*), 'rain' (*charrwaa*) and polite conversation: *tong boo* and *thuche*. I am learning to use a lot of hand gestures; for example, if the sun is out, I can spread my arms into the air and pronounce, "*nyima*"! The hopeful effect, "What a beautiful day!" Saying these few words, I am, at the very least, experimenting with my Sherpa language skills and attempting to be included, in a small way, in the conversation. Phuti churns her own butter in a tall cylindrical structure made of bamboo (I believe, a *dhungro*)—unquestionably strenuous work. She repeatedly suggests that yak butter tea is what I should be drinking; that being said, her words have gone by the wayside as the taste is too strong for me. To be on the safe side, I have also learned a few important words: 'no' (*mengbi*), 'ok' (*las*), and 'it is enough' (*lhangiwi*). Even with my attempts, for the time being, I am unable to take part in any fundamental aspect. I am a guest and treated that way. I could comment (although it is early) that social isolation—verbal as well as musical is confounding—the latter perhaps even more so.

About food, there is only vegetable protein—a nutritious, vegetarian diet, not surprisingly due to the Buddhist culture. Everyone I meet, not to mention this family, seems incredibly strong and exceedingly healthy so the diet must be doing something right. Being not so sure about my robustness and seeing no chickens nearby, I would love a different sort of protein and surmise that if I practice the word for 'eggs' (*chhemendok*) perhaps Phuti can find a few. (I have recruited Mingma and Pasang to check my Sherpa pronunciations—to much laughter!) A great deal of food preparation takes place directly on the floor—no cutting board, just on the floor. Phuti squats as she slices and peels. I am not allowed in this endeavor; she tells me, "Phuti's kitchen." Mingma and Pasang derive great enjoyment from leaving potatoes out for very small roaches to eat. These not-so-enjoyable insects make their home on the sides of the hearth, taking issue with the known concept that roaches usually hide in the daytime. All in all, the girls' efforts are rather sweet responses to the Buddhist philosophy about not harming any sentient beings. Nevertheless, thankfully, Phuti maintains a spick and span kitchen. Pertaining to the western obsession with disinfectants and plastics (none of either exists in this household), it is remarkable to see what is truly necessary.

Starting a fire is still a dilemma. A cup of tea that I have created myself because of a blazing conflagration would be so wondrous. In any event, there seems to be quite a technique I must learn in order to have success with the wooden bellows. The result of my efforts is always either too much air or too little. There is much to learn.

By the end of the first full week, monsoon weather has still not abated. In the afternoon, leaden, dark clouds begin pouring up the river from the south; and in a heartbeat, encompass the entire valley. The windows look out on grayness, and a damp chill takes over the house. Accompanying the low temperature is the earthy smell of rain. The gloom eventually summons bedtime—no electricity, therefore time to turn in. My little room and the sleeping bag provide warmth and comfort. Thankfully, my internal clock has adjusted so that an outhouse trek in the dark (not to mention the rain) can be usually avoided; therefore, one challenge has been accomplished and removed from the list. Tshering previously mentioned that the bad weather may persist for the month, so I intend to take advantage of the monsoon timeline (clouds and rain in the mid afternoon and evening with clouds lifting at daybreak) to hike after morning tea, yet always staying away from the high paths. A favorite walk is to the picturesque waterfall further up the hill, the water tumbling down over a rocky bed whereupon Phuti washes clothes on the stones when necessary. On one occasion, even little Mingma was helping her mother, putting the wet clothing on the rocks of neighboring walls to dry.

A second waterfall lies a little beyond. I did not realize when I arrived in Sengma that this waterfall and stream, a waterway running down a small ravine that showed every sign of being impassable, will become my nemesis. I am not sure when it occurred, but another mudslide has destroyed the bridge we crossed that first day. Because of this event, the only route to the neighboring towns north across the Dudh Kosi (or to Lukla) is to traverse this second body of water (I am sure that to a Sherpa it qualifies as a mere trickle). If I can hike to these small villages, there may be hope of meeting trekkers with whom I can chat, finding books to read, and buying something to eat that is not of a healthy, vegan variety. Crossing this stream is now added to the list of challenges to overcome: becoming proficient with the bellows, washing clothes (and myself)— the list is building quickly. Knowing myself, why will I attempt to tackle the stream alone? It is likely several reasons: my natural inclination to solve a challenge by myself, the difficulty of using the language to ask for help (in my defense, the people in the settlement are always busy in their own pursuits), and perhaps even embarrassment to show weakness—that I am afraid. I am afraid as this experience has proven to be unlike anything that has been before. It is all new. I am truly worried about hurting myself; it certainly seems as though I am far away from any medical help. In addition, being afraid also means to me a feeling of being anxious; and anxious I am—the list is long. In any case, seeing the little settlement of Ghat in the distance, I know that one day I will be there.

During my hikes on the mountain, I sometimes see men leading the hybrid cattle—the animals often burdened with loads of wood and construction materials. The women of Sengma are usually outside their homes working in the gardens. Invariably, they invite me in for a cup of black tea (always strong and warming in the chilly, often damp atmosphere). Because my Sherpa language skills are too minimal to hold any type of a cogent conversation, I resort to my fallback position by utilizing a great number of hand motions and, when not gesturing, sit while they hold a conversation with me. I wish I understood. The other Sengma homes are arranged in the identical Sherpa layout, nevertheless, are usually contrasting in detail. Some have dusty floors instead of wood, concrete instead of stone walls, crude, or tidy hearths, and are often smaller in dimension than Phuti's. The one constant: the smiles and the delight in welcoming a visitor.

As I love projects with a purpose, and with my trusty little camera, I decide to make a 'Path Project'—one that will memorialize the pathways of my hiking expeditions. The following designations I often say out loud as if walking with a friend, wanting to express my surprise at being confronted by these walkways. Some titles depict hardships, others, a normal course of progressing from one place to another. I also became very creative in venturing forth. Not unlike crossing the formidable stream, the brainstorming of the course of action was almost more interesting than the actual accomplishment.

- "Where IS the path?" My general saying of the undefinable.
- "Scenic path." Culminating in a view, often breathtaking, no matter what is underfoot.
- "I don't think so path." Feeling of danger ahead, often relegated to another day.
- "Way too crowded path." Unmoving cattle, this path being the second most common.
- "Ingenious path." Clever use of stones that are not to be categorized as steps, often the only path down or up the inclines.
- "You gotta be kidding path." Deep mud and yet the only way forward—the most common of all the paths.

Sengma, and the mountain upon which it resides, is providing an abundance of unforgettable moments. Pemba wrote a beautiful book, *Bridging Worlds...A Sherpa's Story*. About his home, Pemba wrote: "Despite the poverty and hardships of living in Khumbu, Sengma was a wonderful place to grow up. Very few foreigners visited the area, and it still had the feel of an isolated Sherpa kingdom. Strong family relations are important in Sherpa culture, and I was very close to my siblings and mother. Back then, people tended to remain in the village where they were born without the expectation of ever leaving. We were happy with what we had, perhaps because we knew no other way of life. Growing up in Sengma made me appreciate the simplicity of life and meeting the basic needs of food, shelter, and clothing. There were few complications beyond that."[13]

---

13   Sherpa, Pemba, with James McVey, *Bridging Worlds, A Sherpa's Story*, Sherpa Publications,   2019, 13.

Now, the rhythm in Sengma is exactly that: simple—an easy succession of days. As in Bach's first cello suite, there exists a hopefulness and reassurance that says, "yes, I can be optimistic as well."

TRADITIONS
Doluka-Natang—डोलुक-नाताङ

The days march on—but slowly. To bed at 7:30, up at six or seven. With Phuti lighting juniper incense on the altar every morning, the aroma is not only invigorating but comforting for surely the deities will be looking after me. Little Pasang often stands on a stool to arrange the statues on the altar from place to place. At the age of five, this activity is probably more for fun than deep thought, but I have no idea what is possible.

The monsoon season is still upon us. At times, it is so foggy and rainy that I am unable to see the lower, or upper houses although they are so close. The monsoon's daily schedule has not altered—the days beginning with an almost cloudless blue sky with the white-topped mountains across the valley in full view. In the mid-afternoon when the rain and clouds come from the south, the fog, always accompanied by the rain, gloomily enshrouds all. I am unshakeable in my hope that if the rainy season continues through September, it will end by the beginning of October. I await with enthusiasm for perpetual, beautiful skies just around the corner. Thinking about the trekkers who were on the flight from Kathmandu, I wonder how they are all faring. The best possible time to climb in the Himalayas is known to be in May or before the monsoon season; the other prime time is after the rains cease.

If the rainy weather continues into October, those young trekkers may have missed the opportunity due to the advancing cold.

The trekkers are not the only ones with a possible problem. With the dry weather of winter comes the fear of the cello's sensitive wood cracking. Dryness not being a problem now, even though all string instruments love humidity, I am not convinced that the monsoon season and glue are mutually exclusive. The cello already has a small open seam between the top and one side—the glue has evidently deteriorated.[14] Loving the humidity, the wood of this instrument often swells with the dampness. Thinking that the opening might expand itself shut, the best course of action would be to watch and wait before trying to do some repair work. I did, luckily, remember to bring some clamps and glue in case of a situation like this one. I also brought a few other necessities: resin, needed on the bow; new strings as they break periodically; an alternate bridge (the possibility of a bridge coming asunder is a bit of over-planning); and finally, a tuner to find the right pitch. With this equipment, I am prepared for almost anything.

After the first week in Sengma, and having made great progress on the first suite, my schedule shows that it is the moment to begin Suite II; at the same time, I will continue to explore the very difficult movements of Suite VI, a recurring part of my plan. Not wanting to languish in a sea of self-pity (although I must admit that I have been consumed with feeling sorrowful), the second suite seems appropriate at this moment—in parallel to the daily, morose environment outside the house. This suite is in the key of D minor—a key of anxiety and grief, with a feeling of an introverted sadness. There are techniques I can use to further dramatize or amplify the feeling—less vibrato, a little on the flat side in terms of intonation; both will help to signify sadness. The first movement, the Prelude, begins with a d minor chord, then rises in sorrow (perhaps even anguish) for three measures before falling to the beginning note—a certain capitulation.

---

14 With all violins, violas and cellos, the top table of spruce is glued to the sides, the ribs; the ribs also glued to the back of maple.

After this point, the music does not surrender to defeat but begins to explore solutions—a narrative of my life in Sengma. The realization that I cannot give into defeat has been almost a positive in moving through the day—it certainly is giving me purpose. On a certain level I thought I knew these works; I am finding, however, that what Bach has to teach me about life could be invaluable.

When I spoke about this journey prior to leaving, I stressed the importance of freeing myself of distraction, at the time not knowing if this freedom would be possible. In Sengma, it can be deadly quiet in terms of outside interference. Playing in my tiny room with as much concentration and focus as I can muster, I am finding that not having distraction is a distraction unto itself. This is because the unusual surrounds me in Sengma—the unusual becomes the noise. To thwart this, I am doing my best to involve myself in the life of this Sherpa family to minimize this unsettling effect. Silence in terms of the absence of sound is a reality; I am, however, not isolated from disturbance or intrusion of thought.

Wanting to delve into the idea of meditating while I am memorizing the suites, I decide to put the waterfall across the valley to the test. Using the fall as a focal point (from my viewpoint, it seems to be insanely small), I determine not to think of the fingers of my left hand or the bow (the technique of both requiring thought in a multitude of directions concurrently) but bringing the mind back to my breathing—submerging myself in the music. The active mental exercise of remembering what comes next on a technical level is forced to go by the wayside. Less active recollection, more instinctive recall, is taking place. Even if I am only slightly successful (the mind being quiet as the body is in physical motion), the process is fascinating and may be valuable in the process. The 'out of the ordinary' could become a normal, customary action.

I have a last thought about memorization. If I am faced with a bowing that is completely unnatural to my physicality and to what I am trying to express, the passage is impossible to put to memory. In other words, the bowing that I finally decide upon should be the result of the idea I am trying to express. Bach, in his writing, is always giving us choices. The result (my interpretation) will be because of the options that I choose and that speak to me. If convincing, then the music will convey meaning to the listener.

Although I wanted to bring many books with me on this journey, space did not allow. I did bring one that I thought could give me some insight into the focus required in meditation, the Dalai Lama's *Path to Bliss: A Practical Guide to Stages of Meditation*.[15] It is a work with definite analogies to studying and teaching. Since arriving in Nepal, it has been almost memorized. It is time for another book to read in those minutes after I have wrapped up my practice for the day, and when the weather is not conducive to a hike. I could have guessed that there would be a problem; that although reading materials are in high demand by trekkers, books will be very challenging to track down. I am just not on the right side of the river. Miniature figures of trekkers can be seen across the river, plodding steadily along the faraway path in a long line to Everest and the other mountains on the border of Nepal and Tibet. Porters with loads on their backs, yaks, sherpas and hikers with backpacks— without a doubt, someone has a book. I come to a decision that Ghat, no more than a couple of miles north, is the nearest village of some size where I could find something to read in English. A book possibly dropped off at one of the numerous tea houses along the route would be optimum—a book no longer needed, already read, and occupying space in the backpack.

---

15 Dalai Lama XIV, *The Path to Bliss: A Practical Guide to Stages of Meditation*, Snow Lion Publications, 1991.

Unfortunately, for me to journey north on my side of the valley and to cross the bridge to Ghat, something tells me that I must find a way across that confounding waterfall, the one that cascades over rocks of all sizes and is completely terrifying—the sound of the water rushing down the mountain being fearsome enough. Phuti has pointed to (or, in the direction of) a path leading north on the other side of the stream. At the time, I nodded and said I understood, 'OK' (*las*); however, the trail, upon investigation, looks nonexistent. Any path on the opposite, very steep side of this small ravine is blocked from view due to the massive number of bushes and small trees that are massed together along its entire breadth. After having made quite a few attempts to cross the stream (I figure that finding the trail can come later), the rocks underfoot are decidedly too slippery—too dangerous for me to wade across. Admittedly, I am also being a very cautious coward, not wanting an injury in this early part of the trip.

Never one to give up and not surrendering to defeat (the idea of reaching Ghat was too enticing), I begin to go to the stream every day, placing ever larger, flat stones into the gully, hoping to gradually build a path over the rushing water that would be crossable. I found a board that became a bed for some stones, but my engineering skills are no match for this seemingly hopeless action. I am determined to find a solution. There was no one I could really ask for help as any self-respecting Sherpa would think it ridiculous that I cannot just run through the water to the other side (and they would be wearing flip-flops no less). Thankfully, no one seems to be watching as I throw more and more stones into the stream. Even if they were watching in complete disbelief, I doubt that anyone would feel it necessary to give me some logs or suggestions to help. As far as they know, I am just enjoying myself—playing in the water. I am imagining this, of course; and the imaginary stone bridge I have in my mind is gradually becoming a reality—a tangible passage. I have decided more than once during the early days of this adventure that part of this journey is to be self-sufficient. At times it just seems too difficult—primarily because I want it so much.

This entire community provides lessons in self-sufficiency. Along with the homes on the mountain, there are a few other little structures, some of which I have never entered. I ventured into one, a little hut made of stones settled into the hillside, housing an old grindstone. I could hazard a guess that it is for wheat, after harvesting. On my way to the stream, I often stop to spend some time in another building, a *gompa* of sorts, but perhaps it is more of a meditation room in substance. This structure contains a large, floor-to-ceiling, beautifully engraved, and colorful prayer wheel along with numerous pots and statues. I turn the wheel for a few minutes, saying my own prayer to whomever is listening, hoping for good days ahead. Tshering, as we had turned the prayer wheels in Chaurikharka, had told me that the sherpa, in rotating a prayer wheel over and over is, in effect, chanting *mantras* hundreds of times. In Sengma I find, if others are in the wheelhouse with me, they are in constant conversation with one another rather than in meditative thought. Concentration seems divided; but then, I am an outsider and do not understand the words shared. Mingma, once when we were walking together, produced a few sounds with a conch shell (the voice of the Buddha), the shell found on a shelf along with other statuary. Every day I am struck with the beauty of traditions. I say to myself that stopping to turn the wheel before placing a few more rocks into the stream must help.

Today, September 22, in the wee hours of the morning before my customary hike, I am perching on a stone wall in front of the house, contemplating Lukla in the far distance. Doing this either makes me homesick (I would love to be in one of those little planes taking off) or is comforting (I know the possibility to return to Lukla is there—just a hike to Ghat and then south). I have been in Nepal for greater than two weeks, and my mind shows every sign of being incessantly on the trip home. Having a phone conversation or sending a message to friends and family to let them know that all is alright and that I have survived the first couple of weeks, could possibly make all the difference. Then, unquestionably, I could breathe somewhat easier. I must remind myself that the length of time in Sengma is a window of opportunity for reflection. Importantly, the situation in which I find myself is a journey for which I have thoroughly prepared; and even though full of doubt and anxiety, I may never have the opportunity to repeat an adventure such as this one again. Using the time well is of primary importance. There are many extraordinary things happening each day that I want to commit to memory along with the one constancy—Bach.

School is evidently 'open' for the youngsters on this side of the river. Mingma and Pasang seem to have a haphazard schedule of attendance. Today, Mingma asked me if I would like to see the school, so we hike up the mountain to a low, simple stone structure with a wood floor and benches for sitting, tables for their notebooks. The building is quite a distance from the house along a muddy and rocky path, high on the neighboring hill. (In hindsight, thinking of the young boys in red sweaters and caps in Lukla, I wonder if the girls trekked to this building due to the destruction of the bridge leading to Lukla.) Every morning, from their house window, Mingma and Pasang watch for the teacher coming in the distance, probably from Ghat. When he is in view (the equivalent of the bell being rung), they grab their notebooks and head up to the school. During the days when the teacher has not arrived, they devise many activities to keep busy, all pursued with great smiles and laughter. When I am practicing, they do their very best to disturb me; in their way, asking me to join them in their projects. My concentration can be completely halted when chatter and small faces arrive at the window of my room (as the house is set on the hill, my window on the second floor is easily accessible). They continue with an uproar until I surrender. As all young children love singing games, I have taught the girls a couple of tried-and-true favorites. I have a limited repertoire, but two nursery rhymes, *Itsy Bitsy Spider*[16] and *London Bridge*,[17] are big hits—a few Sherpa words in translation!

---

16 North, Arthur Walbridge, *Camp and Camino in Lower California*. New York: The Baker & Taylor Company, 1910, pp. 279–280.

17 English nursery rhyme, the earliest records of the rhyme in English are from the 17th century. https://en.wikipedia.org/wiki/London_Bridge_Is_Falling_Down.

ITSY BITSY SPIDER
Lyrics using some Sherpa from the dictionary,
taught along with the hand motions!

Tikpe, tikpe bu – went up the kangbaa,
Down came chawaa and washed the bu out!
Out came nyima and dried up all the chawaa,
Then the tikpe, tikpe bu, went up the kangbaa again!

Mingma and Pasang also want to learn a bit of English. With my Sherpa dictionary I can translate a few Sherpa words, generally accurately, into English. I appreciate that they are learning at school even if their education is rather unstructured! Today I took a lovely photo of Pasang saying, "Oh, my gosh!" with a surprised look—not a necessary expression for existence, but it was fun teaching the motion and trying to explain that something has happened, and she is amazed!

I rarely see Phuti for she is either outside working in the fields or she has left for parts unknown. My observation is that she is a solemn and introspective person—serious in her interaction with the two girls, serious about the household, and serious about her labor on the land. For Phuti, I would say 75% of the day is spent in preparing food, either working in or collecting vegetables from the fields or cooking the daily meals. When I offer to help in preparing food or any of her tasks, Phuti laughs: "Phuti's food; Phuti's washing." In addition, Sherpa women do seem to be 'masters of the fire,' especially in contrast to my pitiful attempts in pursuance of lighting a piece of wood. Until food has been assembled and put on the fire, it is oftentimes difficult to watch the preparation.

Potatoes are stored down below in the cattle stalls, then peeled and prepared in what presents itself as rather cloudy water. This readying of vegetables for the fire is always accomplished squatting (while chopping) on the floor even though some space on the hearth is available. There is no refrigeration, so food is left out—even leftovers from the meal before. Pots and pans are not washed until they are to be used again. The roaches are still disquieting; but they are small and in contrast to everything else, they seem insignificant.

At other times, Phuti occupies herself with usual activities: washing clothes (accomplished on Sunday in the stream, using the rocks for scrubbing), taking care of the girls (Phuti is often looking in the girls' hair. I wonder if for lice?), cleaning the living space (she throws water on the floor before sweeping), and, importantly, conversing with neighbors outdoors, the women often calling from house to house—a make-shift telephone service! Along with the other men and women in the village, she usually wears either flip-flops or sneakers, the former a surprise on this mountainous terrain.

I feel as though I am watching the life around me as if in a cinema. I know that I am a 'guest,' however having people around me, having everyone involved in life and yet keeping a formal distance—I am finding that difficult. As time moves on, I am feeling more the isolation— the isolation of not being able to communicate in any meaningful way, the isolation of not being able to share my music, and the isolation due to the lack of closeness with those around me. The Tibetan cell would, in many ways, have been easier.

A few thoughts about that life 'around me.' In general, the Sherpa people are patient and sharing—spending their day in hard, physical labor. The men—most of whom work for trekking companies based in Kathmandu, find this occupation to be full-time, difficult, and dangerous. We know the stories told of Sherpas who, in paving the way for climbers to reach the 'top', have died on climbing expeditions, in some instances along with their clients. Older men in the villages, along with the women and those men who have decided against joining the trekking community, remain on the land and seem to oversee the cattle and work the fields, planting in the spring and harvesting in the summer and fall. For the Sherpa, farming has been the way of life for hundreds of years.

I am seeing first-hand how this village is reliant upon the land—that food must be available, not only for the family but for the cattle in the difficult months of winter. Grass for the animals is brought down from the mountains, dried on the fields, covered up when it rains, and then spread out again when the weather clears—the process repeated over and over. Food is grown on the surrounding fields—the potato (*riki*) and wheat seem to be the most important crops, milk and water are plentiful; and if clothing is needed, it is brought back from Kathmandu. Foreign clients often leave behind items that can be used by their guides and porters and their families, especially clothing—a custom at the conclusion of a trek. With so little, everyone manages with what they already have. In terms of material possessions, there is little—if not available and necessary, it does not exist.

Personal hygiene seems to take place for the same reason—when it is necessary. Mingma and Pasang have a bath every Saturday in a large bowl on the floor. Seeing Mingma giving Pasang a bath is a vision I will never forget! I make use of the bowl and hot water as often as possible, although the entire procedure becomes a bit of a chore. I can see that going without a shower for these three months will be eye-opening—I doubt I will even care. Cleanliness is rather low on my list of vitally important activities to accomplish.

Phuti's husband, Chongba, is home! He has been leading a trek in the Annapurna region—the Annapurna being one of the highest mountains in the world. It is wonderful to finally become acquainted with the fourth member of this little family. Unfortunately, he is home for only a day or two as another trek will soon begin. Chongba, a handsome young man, looks quite up to date—wearing western clothing and trendy hiking shoes. Along with farming the land, the lifestyle and business of leading Westerners on treks and climbing in the high mountains is an important, albeit dangerous, sideline.

As Chongba speaks English as does his brother, Pemba, I have a chance to talk to him about his life, the life that I can only observe from a visitor's distance. The day after he returned, Chongba, Pasang and I went on a short hike down the mountain. We sat together on a large, flat rock before heading back to the house. He spoke about his arranged marriage with Phuti around their age of 22. For his own children, Chongba is not sure if this tradition should continue. He said, "More and more the girls are influenced by Western culture; they may want to marry for love." I hope that I can see the girls in twenty years to see how they are faring. As we were sitting, little Pasang came and sat on Chongba's knee. This small act seemed so simple at the time—a true poignant moment. It was surprising because in the time I have spent with Phuti and the girls, this sort of closeness—the parent relationship to the child, has not included a great deal of touching. The girls tend to shy away from me if I put my hand on them in any way; for example, they had to be almost bribed to hold hands in the singing game, *London Bridge*. I know that the Nepali way does not include much touching; I assume it must be similar in the Sherpa culture. Making a small effort in teaching the girls a few little songs and, for example, the word for 'hug' and what it means, I am trying to overcome the separateness between us while trying to respect their feelings.

It is now almost the end of the first month. The loneliness is palpable for I long for anything new to happen. My schedule is remaining the same: breakfast, hike, lunch, practice, and relaxing outside before supper if the rain is delayed (this is the time when the girls like to entertain). There is a real rhythm to the day, but the rhythm is slow and unforgiving—Cavatina-like.[18] In the late afternoon the clouds usually return to rain all night and clear once again in the morning.

Chongba has left once again; however, the family has been augmented by a new person—a young man from Nepal, Tika. He is welcome in a fashion that indicates that he has been here

---

18   A reference to *String Quartet, Op. 130* by Beethoven, the *Cavatina* movement.

before to help in the fields when it is time for the threshing of grain and hoeing of the plot of land. The area surrounding the homes in Sengma is generally quite hilly, requiring the *yuk-yaks* to be harnessed to a slightly crude, but very effective plow—a wooden apparatus constructed with sturdy tree branches. During this month, Phuti has been spending the days with her neighbors, hoeing the plots by hand. Now is the time for help; this is where Tika comes in.

In threshing the grain Tika is using another interesting handmade wooden tool. About six feet in length, it has a long handle with movable lower sticks.

Tika gave it to me to try, however the technique of swinging this unwieldy instrument was a bit too complex, it being impossible to swing and thresh anything on the ground. The idea that Tika asked me to try the tool was unlike anything asked before. Even now, almost a month after I arrived, when I offer to dig potatoes alongside Phuti in the field, as in cooking or cleaning, I was met with a quick rebuke, "Phuti's work." Watching and listening to the activity happening around me, realizing that the work is done only to survive the cold, harsh winter months, I praise the ingenuity and steadfastness of the Sherpa people.

When I was a young girl (we moved from Toronto to Alabama in the '50's), farming was not an unknown lifestyle. My father, besides his life in music, was an English gentleman farmer. We lived in the country on quite a few acres that were cultivated primarily with acres of corn and other typical southern vegetables: beans, carrots, and collard greens. We had two cows (Ruben and Rachel), two pigs (Dad knew better than to let us get attached with naming these two as they did mysteriously leave one day, never to return), and quite a few chickens. My father worked hard in the fields as his father had done before him in the fields of Sussex, England; so, I did understand the life. Even loving the outdoors and the entire process of farming, we did, however, have the good fortune of owning a modern tractor and tools. Because of that upbringing, I still love gardening today. I let no one take care of the few indoor plants I own: "Judy's plants."

I would love to help Phuti or Tika in the fields. Tika tended to be in the house one minute, working on the hillside the next, and then, like Phuti, he would be gone. Tika spoke Nepali while Phuti and the girls, even though understanding Nepali, spoke Sherpa. Not comprehending either language, I tried not to concentrate on all that I was missing. Instead, I enjoyed the new sounds and sometimes raucous musicality of both languages. One evening, Tika made a speaker for a little, damaged radio he had found. He put this old, tiny speaker inside a plastic peanut butter jar, ran a cord outside for an antenna and hung the entire contraption on the ceiling. Nepali pop songs were streaming out of this little radio while Mingma danced, moving all over the floor with little Pasang trying to keep up. I was slightly offended that I was enjoying their music, however at no time did they want to listen to mine. Petty, I know; but these are desperate times. It was wonderful to see the smiling faces of those two little girls light up the room with their dancing! Unfortunately, when he left the next day, Tika took the radio with him.

PART THREE

PART THREE

SURRENDER
Tong-jka तोग जक

The bridge over the stream, my only escape to the north, is almost finished. I am beginning to see the point where I will make the cross-over. The result of my handiwork is quite remarkable—an engineering model of excellence! A few more days, and I will have completed all that is required.

Alongside the breathtaking possibility of the new hike to Ghat, I have arrived at the C Major Suite, Bach's third suite in this group of six. The music is propped up on my backpack against the wooden wall. The mood of this suite is confident, the first bar stating the complete C Major scale without a hint of doubt or pessimism—the scale is open and honest in its simplicity. When I began working on the first two suites, the timing had been parallel to my experience and thought process here in Sengma. The third suite, with its positive nature, will remain parallel as I am planning to use the suite to direct me on a new path—one that is settled and decisive with the result being one of joy and happiness. At the beginning of the suite, Bach is stating, "I am determined in my conviction."

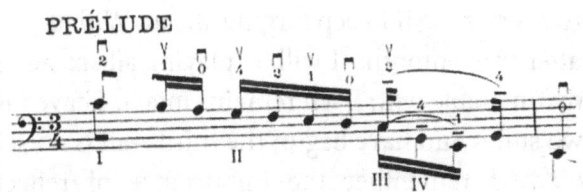

To be determined in taking this new path, I must push away the constant emptiness—the blankness that is a result of watching, as an observer, the scene move past. Even though I know that in Sengma nothing will change in any remarkable way, I want the simple actions of everyday life that I am observing to be meaningful and to change something within myself. The few moments of participating in life here have not been enough. At times I have felt that I am just sitting and waiting. Waiting for it all to end is unpleasant and defeatist. True, I am lonely and at times, very sad; that being said, for the two months left I have two choices: continue to watch it all go by or burst out and experience the fullness of life here in Sengma as best I can.

My primary goal, of course, is to relearn all six suites. As I move to the last four, however, the technique and musicality of the works are becoming increasingly more difficult. Because of the route I have taken in life, I have always expected demanding trials, most of them being musical—performing difficult works either alone or with others. To overcome these challenges, I have been able, when necessary, to 'pull out of the hat' certain tools—those having to do with the physical playing of the instrument developed since I was young. It is time to pull out all the stops in playing the suites and in my overall existence here in Nepal. The tools I have in my possession to learn the suites as their difficulty increases are the same tools I need to move forward—those of purpose, commitment, and perseverance. I will cross the stream.

Almost a month in Sengma, and I have decided to surrender, to concede that anything is possible in Khumbu. Even though it is difficult to shake the feeling that the dreariness is too much, there is meaning to everything if I keep forging ahead. With determination in mind, after three months, I will be playing all six suites without a break. My timetable with Bach remains intact. I have memorized the first two suites and have begun the third—all is on schedule.

Every day I remember the importance of reflection and simplicity. I am learning, in small or large events, how little we really need. This morning I looked outside to see Mingma and

Pasang playing house. Mingma was fiddling with a cup on the stone wall; little Pasang was rocking her doll—a splintered piece of wood wrapped in a filthy scrap of cloth—cradled in her arms as if the most prized possession. Another lesson to be taken home from Sengma—I do not need very much to have a good and satisfactory life. One day Pasang may have a real doll to play with; in the meantime, seeing her smile, I knew that the doll being a piece of wood made no difference.

Chongba has been in Kathmandu with hikers after returning from the mountains. I had asked him to check, while in Kathmandu, to see if Dinesh has any mail for me. He had planned to return before leaving again for another expedition; however, he was delayed being unable to confirm his seat on the plane to Lukla. In climbing the mountains in the Himalaya, the two best climbing periods are late spring and early fall—the Sherpa livelihood dependent upon this timing. If delayed for too long a period, the repercussions could be great. Luckily, he arrives the next day with an email from a California friend and one from Tshering. The correspondence confirms that the outside actually exists! In the distance, I still look at the planes flying in and out of Lukla. After hearing Chongba's story of no seat being available, I am already wondering, even two months ahead, if the trip back to Kathmandu will actually happen on the date stamped on my government form.

Pasang has cut her chin playing outside. It is a large gash that in the States would require stitches. I have antiseptic and band-aids to give her although Phuti does not seem to be too concerned. When someone is frightfully ill in Sengma or breaks a bone, the closest medical care would be in Namche Bazaar, a large town on the trek to Everest—a long day's walk if not more. If extremely serious, a flight from Lukla to Kathmandu would be necessary. A very long hike or a plane flight—it is hard to imagine having to make that choice. If faced with those two options, I imagine it is easier to ignore anything that is not life-threatening. I wonder about vaccines for preventative medicine, if these are available and part of the Sherpa experience.

The big moment has happened! It took a month, but I crossed the stream! To summarize, I kept placing and layering those stones in the stream. While the possibility of slipping on the wet, slick rocks was still a palpable threat, I gingerly stepped over my newly constructed bridge. Perhaps 'threat' is too strong a word, but I know without a doubt that this stream has the intent to do me harm. Even now, with the building of an equivalent to the Brooklyn Bridge over this small waterway, I was still fearful and crossed very slowly.

Once across the bridge, I followed a narrow path along the ravine until the worn pathway simply ended. The trail must continue at the top of this ridge to my left. From my standpoint, the route upward was covered with bushes making it indistinguishable. I was a trifle confused. If this is how everyone goes to Ghat, why isn't the trail more definable? There must be another path that is more obvious; but, for the moment, I will make this route my own. I clambered up and pulled myself over the ridge, using the branches of nearby bushes. Cannot anything be easy? Do I have to build a ladder out of branches now? Once over the top, I saw a possible trail, not well-worn but walkable. Pulling some of the undergrowth out of the way to make the climb easier next time, I walked onwards, completely satisfied with this new accomplishment. I am also convinced that the next attempt will be easier, although the ladder idea seems a good one. As I stepped onward, surrounded by trees and undergrowth, two small, golden monkeys watched, and then followed my progress. The little macaques chattered in a high-pitched squeal but remained on the side of the trail, not hindering my movement forward. I passed a few houses—women outside in their gardens, but I was too eager and excited to see what was on the other side of the Dudh Kosi to stop and say 'hello'.

Even though Phuti could probably complete this hike in 10 minutes, it took me over an hour to arrive at the bridge leading into Ghat. This bridge is in much better shape than the bridge I originally crossed over the river. It is a solid, wooden structure with wooden railings instead of ropes (very comforting). Thankfully, I could not see the river below me through the plank flooring. A clever construction, at either end the supports are simply huge rocks piled on top of each other (not so comforting, but at this point, there is not a better bridge to be found).

In Ghat, I stopped at a small shop connected to the local teahouse. With a Coke in my hand (OMG! A drink other than water and tea!) I found a paperback book in English on a small little table—*The Viconte de Bragelonne* by Dumas. It had evidently been left by a trekker to lighten his or her load. I stopped at another little store, buying some bottled water for me and chocolate for us all, only feeling a little guilty about the fact that the dentist is probably a plane ride away. On the path back to the bridge, I met two young English hikers; one had been in a Kathmandu hospital for five days, cause unknown. Another group of nine Swiss people were on their way to climb Cho Oyu—the sixth-highest mountain in the world about 20 kilometers west of Everest. They had a long walk and climb ahead. Another hiker stopped to join the group—a very talkative young man, Peter, from New York who now lives in Cornwall in the UK. He promised to stop by Sengma on the way back to Lukla as he would love to visit a true Sherpa home and village and to hear a little Bach. It would be delightful if he comes; and thinking how exciting it would be to have an English-speaking visitor, I almost had him sign a promissory note. After this initial success in discovering outside life, I will come back often; not only to involve myself with the adventures of trekkers on their way north, but also to meet those in the little settlements on my side of the valley. The feeling of freedom as I began the long hike back, knowing that I had stretched my boundaries for the first time, was indescribable.

On the way home, an elderly woman was standing by her gate, evidently completing some work in her garden—a gigantic display of primrose flowers (in a range of blues—violet and purple). She invited me in for tea; and as I was feeling happy and quite exuberant, not caring about my lack of the language, I followed her into her home. Her husband (I am supposing) is evidently a maker of string instruments! According to the many parts waiting to be assembled, he is evidently a repairer as well. It was a complete surprise to see the instrument he is holding—a beautifully constructed and decorated Nepalese instrument: a bowed, 4-stringed *serenji*.

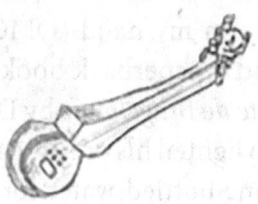

Even more of a surprise was listening to him play. I was struck with the improvisatory beauty and melismatic nature of the tune, no doubt a typical Nepali song.[19] He was a fascinating gentleman with a good technique and a cheerful and joyous personality. As I gain more experience in walking from Sengma to Ghat when I need more chocolate or when I am looking for a book, I look forward to meeting more of the women and men who live in the small villages on the trail north. They will inevitably invite me in for tea (hopefully, of the black variety, and not the thick, sickly yak butter tea). Every minute spent with my new neighbors will be a joy. Being in Ghat, to speak English again and to have a real conversation, was all I needed to call this hike a grand accomplishment. The loneliness I have felt from the lack of communication has been real. This day was extraordinary.

I believe in the deities. Because of my success with the hike to Ghat, we have almost had a full day without clouds, at least not until the late evening. In general, it has become rainy again at night with the added misery of the chill in the air. It is the beginning of October and the advent of fall. I have begun putting a blanket over the cello, thinking it could possibly keep the chill away, but I would think this is a fool's errand. My study of Suite III is coming along well. I almost have the first three suites memorized while I continue work on the difficult movements coming up in the final three. Days are

---

19   To hear a *serenji*: Prince Nepali, *https://www.youtube.com/watch?v=HzKO5CfF5nE*

clicking off in the rhythm of each note I play. I wonder if I will reach a point when I am not thinking about December and the trip back home. This must be what homesickness feels like. The daily schedule remains much the same except for one addition in the afternoon: a tea break with boiled potatoes that Phuti has brought in from the fields. After that afternoon pause, I go for another short hike, supper, and in bed by 6:30 or 7 when the sun goes down. I believe I am finally understanding enough to live the rhythm of the day.

Having had a guest in her house for over a month, Phuti has been very ingenious with her cooking at mealtimes. Different recipes are always produced at breakfast or supper (both being very light meals), and yet the lunch menu is primarily variations of *dal bhat*. This Sherpa staple is easy to prepare and always delicious and spicy containing a large amount of chili sauce. Potato pancakes, *Mai-Ta Toppa* (fat pasta), *Momos* (with cabbage), and Pancakes (with sauteed vegetables) are my ultimate favorites. *Chapati* and *Luma Pourrie* are both rather sweet, and the only dishes I can remember that were not served with chilis! Phuti gave up trying to give me yak butter tea (*su chya*), so black tea has been my beverage of choice. When Tika was visiting, he and Phuti drank an alcoholic drink, *chang*. Made of fermented rice, it is supposed to help altitude sickness or dehydration. I took a sip, and that was enough for me to put *chang* alongside *su chya* as fluids not to swallow.

I feel that it would be terribly easy to become ill, and yet I have been safe so far. To enter Nepal, I was required to have a gamut of vaccines; and, in addition, I brought several naturopathic remedies which seem to have been doing their work. Although everything I eat is either cooked well or boiled, I am still diligent in taking these preventative medicines and have become quite proficient with the water purifier. The environment seems so chancy, especially with the change in diet and, at least to my western sensibility, with the conditions in general.

Walking up to the top house today, I believe the monks have finally left. The Buddhist mourning period for the two lost in the avalanche—the length of time helping them pass into the next life, must be over. "Most Buddhist honor their dead (giving prayers for the deceased) for three, five, or seven days. This is because even numbers are seen as 'complete,' while odd numbers have a sense of 'becoming.' Choosing an odd number of days serves as a reminder that this is a transitional period for the person's *atman* (the soul)."[20] With the idea of numbers being static or mobile, I am reminded of Zoltan Kodaly's hand signals in teaching music. Believing in the importance of singing in music education for young children, Kodaly (a Hungarian composer) used hand motions to describe the pitch: the even pitches (do, mi, so) are stable; the odd pitches (re, fa, la, ti) are leading up or down—they are 'becoming.'[21]

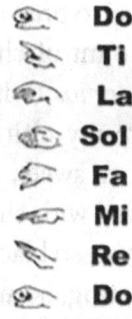

In the same manner that I count the days remaining in Sengma, I am counting the number of Bach movements that are 'complete' or are 'becoming.' Bach is the obsession that rules my day, however there are other preoccupations that, at times, are just as important: to be safe, to find more books, to take one day at a time, to take advantage of the sun being out—the list continues. Just when I think about making the most of every day, I revert and think about the cold, the incessant heavy rain at night, and the possibilities of leaving Sengma in November. When the real winter takes over,

---

20 Better Place Forests, "The Complete Guide to Buddhist burial practices and rituals," 2022, https://www.betterplaceforests.com/blog/articles/the-complete-guide-to-buddhist-burial-practices-and-rituals.
21 Kemp, Allyssa, "Solfège Syllables & Kodály Hand Signals," 2021, https://eastside-music.com/solfege-syllables-kodaly-hand-signals/.

Tshering felt that it would be good to move to a warmer climate, to Nagarkot, about 30 kilometers from Kathmandu. Nagarkot, primarily a Hindu village, sits at the edge of the Kathmandu Valley at over 7,000 feet where the weather is milder and will be easier for the cello to cope (and a change of scenery for me).

Phuti walked to Lukla today. Because the path we came up a month ago is no longer viable due to a second avalanche (the bridge we had originally crossed is no longer there), Phuti had to take the long way north to Ghat and then south to Lukla. It would take me, a normal-paced hiker, at least three hours in total. When she returned late morning, I was stunned—Phuti brought back a huge number of EGGS! This is truly a momentous occasion. (I wonder what suddenly changing my diet will do to my system.) Not giving that last sentence a moment of thought, having longed for eggs, or some other type of protein since I arrived in Sengma, I am suddenly eating eggs every morning, the girls enjoying the new taste sensation as well. Since the eggs arrived, a mercenary side of my personality has unfortunately shown itself—an egoism of which I am not proud. I am being highly protective of these eggs, of trying to convince Mingma and Pasang to have toast instead of MY eggs. My trying to be convincing has been a complete failure. As Phuti is not making use of the eggs in other ways, scrambled or fried (with ample amounts of chili sauce) is simply perfect.

Speaking of Mingma and Pasang, my practicing is on schedule, but the two girls are very noisy. There are few school days, so they are often home, leaving them more opportunity to be irksome. As they are difficult to decipher, I wish I could really speak to them. I say a few words or make motions asking them to be quiet if they are being interruptive, but to no avail; they do not seem to understand what and why I am playing this instrument and wanting peace and quiet. I am sure that Tshering's words to them when I first arrived about the project made no sense at all. They are either too young, think the music bizarre, or are just creatively annoying. For these two little girls, music is a time to dance, to sing, to be exuberant. They are in all probability just as stymied as I am in not being able to communicate. Today they are left by themselves except for me, and I acknowledge that I can be of little guidance. At one point I took a break in my practicing and noticed that Pasang was sitting on the ground outside playing with a rather large machete, the blade at least a foot long—the reason for her chopping on the ground not evident. The motive of my taking away the huge knife was, to her, equally not evident. There are beautifully quiet moments as well; for example, when Mingma is sitting on the bench with her school notebook up against the windowsill. I do love looking over her shoulder, watching her do homework. I ask as many questions as possible as she seems eager to share this activity with me. I still cannot figure out when the girls should be in school, as I do not think their teacher comes very often. I am also not sure how many students climb that hill. One day, I must investigate and walk up to the school when it is (supposed to be) in session.

The imagination of these two little girls has no bounds. As I watch them in their day-to-day life: doing their homework, in the yard playing or helping Phuti at the stream or in the fields, I am conscious of the fact that there are many ways to learn. Mingma and Pasang will be fine no matter how many days the teacher walks down the path and the imaginary bell rings.

It is the beginning of October, and the weather continues—raining all night and clearing up in the morning. During the day, with high clouds still floating above and the fog (mukpaa) moving into the valley in the late afternoon, the beauty of the mountaintops is often obscured. Seeing those clouds march up the valley and then settle around the house is ominous and unsettling. Phuti finally tells me that we can leave soon for Everest; I am hoping (and praying) for the weather to change at long last, for I would love to see unobstructed views as we hike north. The morning sun is perfect for the daily hikes apart from the extreme mud situation along the trails, the sludge produced by the constant rain in the evening. The large shrubs of primrose and rhododendrons are still flowering along the paths; in fact, all plant life seems to be enjoying the wet evenings and the daily blue skies. Adding to this local scenery, the gargantuan snowy mountains that can be seen to the north and to the east when not obscured by the clouds are a magical backdrop on the stage of this play. It is completely breath-taking.

With Bach, I am zipping through I, II, and III with ease. I am being organized with my practice schedule, although at times I wonder if the files in my old brain have been filled—no more space remaining. Belying that fact, the first month in Sengma has been highly successful in terms of memorizing Bach; however, not so much with the meditative aspect. The meditation idea, although a beautiful one to be sure, is gaining traction but still seems to be beyond my grasp. It is still so difficult to be physically busy, and yet keeping my mind free and inactive. This is a work in progress. My latest theory, and one just beginning to feel real, is that the altitude is giving me a lighter sense of the music. I will have to wait until the end of the project to fully grasp this reality, but it is holding fast. As we will soon be departing Sengma for our hike to the Everest region, I will begin suite IV in earnest when Phuti and I return. The fourth suite is in a difficult key (Eb) and thus is awkward for performance (the left hand must solve the problem of not being perennially in a stretch position). I will go slowly, also introducing movements from suites V and VI as I move through IV. Again, this work must wait as another main event is about to begin.

In the cold of the afternoon, as I sit in front of the fire with a cup of tea—sometimes with Phuti and the girls, sometimes alone, I think about this complicated Sherpa family. Through another's eyes this family is intriguing. Pasang is the spoiled one; Mingma—the one who provokes. As I have said, the two girls are sometimes aggressive, hitting each other and their mother. I have told them they cannot hit me, my words attempting to ward off any possibility. Chongba is rarely here, being either in Kathmandu or on the hiking trails. He is a quiet man, seemingly an authoritarian. I have not seen much interaction between Chongba and the girls unless walking outside; but I have not seen a huge amount of, what I would call, misbehaving when he is home. Mingma seems to be timid and apprehensive around him (she sleeps alone on the benches along the wall when Chongba is home—the others sleep together on mats on the floor. Pasang is "daddy's girl."

Surrounded by loving family and friends has been my world—a family of 'huggers.' I have seen little aggression in my life; in fact, I have only seen one person violently hit another, and that incident was in Moscow. I am therefore surprised to see the amount of aggression (a contentious attitude) that exists among a very calm and peaceful people. One afternoon, a young girl in her teens was visiting Sengma. In broken English, she mentioned that once, when she returned home late, her brother got so angry as she was not at home to make lunch and tea, he kicked her. When I told Phuti, she laughed. Not understanding the reaction, I must remember that Nepalis do not like to give a negative as an answer. I was being negative; Phuti was not.

This evening it rained all night, keeping me up for hours. There are evenings when the idea of going to sleep when it is dark (usually around 6:30 or 7) is not going to happen. A special moment, however, is when the rain quiets and I can hear the Dudh Kosi roaring down the valley. This is not morose as is the rain; this is the sound of the energy from Everest—the Goddess of the Sky has come alive. The trails for my usual walks become quite dangerous when wet; however, staying inside my little room, or even in the house alone, is often unbearable; the saving grace—sitting with my cello in the throes of Bach. The first suite alone, that suite in the smiling key of G Major, has the capability of making it all tolerable. Smelling the green of the land and exercising up and down the hills is a welcome event in my everyday life as well—every hike continues to be an adventure. Adding to these walks, it is extraordinary to take part, if only as an observer, in the new activities attributable to the coming of fall—the men cutting grass and the women hoeing in the nearby fields. It is all very peaceful for little has changed in the way of life, at least on the farmland, for hundreds of years.

I have received a few letters and emails for which I am so very thankful. These come from Kathmandu by plane, then a runner (always seems to be Dowa, a very energetic young fellow) arriving in Sengma. Always amazed and in words I have said many times, I am sure that Dowa, who delivers mail and news, runs the distance (Lukla to Ghat and across the river to Sengma), conquering the terrain in a very short amount of time. When days go by without any news from home, I am thankful for an incredibly special little book—a tiny volume only 1 ½" x 2" given to me by a wonderful student, Summer. She went to the time-consuming effort of creating an absolute treasure by gluing to the pages of the book extremely miniaturized copies of the Bach preludes. In addition, my friends and students wrote (it goes without saying in tiny script), messages of encouragement: "Play loudly," "Peace, love, Bach," "Be safe and come back soon!" As I was soon to discover, the number of times that I glanced through those pages reading the well-wishes from my remarkable friends in Boulder, saved me on many occasions.

Finally, on October 4, Phuti tells me that we can leave for Mount Everest in two days. The trek is happening! Everest has been unrivalled in the number one position on my bucket list—not to reach the summit, of course, but it is enough to view and reflect upon its emotional and spiritual impact. Tika is going to return to stay with Mingma and Pasang while Phuti and I go north. We will leave for Namche Bazar, a village at over 11,000 feet which is the main resting stop for trekkers going to the Mount Everest massif and to the mountains further north. Climbers will usually rest in Namche for two or three days to acclimatize for the attempts to climb higher; in addition, it is their last outpost to acquire any equipment or food necessary for what lies ahead.

Thinking that I was a mountain climber in a previous life, I may have been a good mountaineer if my interest, at a younger age, had moved me in that direction. Growing up in a musical family with strong and unflappable parents, studying the cello with my mother until leaving to study in college and having two sisters who studied violin with my father, playing and performing chamber music with my family was a natural and joyous way of life. Mountain climbing was not in the forecast; and, for now, I will just enjoy the view.

Unlike those who are making the attempt, Phuti and I will only go as far as Namche, spending an evening or two before returning home. From this village, if we hike another hour along the hikers' trail that goes to Everest's South Base Camp (the northern base camp is in Tibet), Phuti tells me that on a clear day, Everest, the Lhotse Nuptse Ridge, Ama Dablam, and the other high peaks that make up the High Himalaya can be seen. I recognize the name of Ama Dablam. Over 22,000 feet, this mountain is often climbed after the monsoon season has ended as there is less snow and more rock and ice (someone other than me must explain that one). Since it is October and many climbers are already in Namche preparing for ascents, those we encounter along the trail will no doubt be hikers (like me) wanting to breathe the air on the way to see the top of the world. Trying to keep in training for the upcoming, adventurous hike, I often walk as quickly as possible up the mountain behind the house, but always keeping the boundary of the tiger's sanctuary in mind. It would be a tragedy if the clouds completely covered Everest when at Namche; however, it will be glorious to get away to stretch myself mentally and physically in this upcoming challenge.

We will be gone for about 6 days. The trek to Sagarmatha National Park, the area dominated by Mount Everest, will take us across to Ghat and then to little villages further north—Phakding and Jorsale, arriving at Namche Bazar the second day of the trip. I would also like to visit Khumjung, a little north of Namche, to see Edmund Hillary's school that he built in 1961 for the Sherpa children. Today in Sengma, however, by mid-afternoon the weather has gradually deteriorated from a sunny sky to pouring rain. This rain will never stop. Even with the promise of really bad weather for this hike, I need a change from the monotonous schedule I have religiously been keeping. Although I am appreciative of this family and those in the village opening their homes and lives to me, the living conditions are tiring. The overarching isolation, darkness and the coming cold of winter is very challenging. Being so socially isolated is creating a numbness, a desolation that at times overrides all. Thinking back to my original idea, having food slid under the door in a Tibetan monastery, I laugh at my naiveté in thinking I could have mentally survived the rather extreme conditions of living in a small cell. Pondering all of this, today is not a good day for enjoying Sherpa living. The weather is relentless in its monotony.

The day before we leave, I play through Suites I, II and III, hoping that not a great deal will be forgotten by the time I return. The sun is thankfully out this morning bringing several men (they just suddenly appear and then disappear) to work in the hills, cutting and gathering grass. I hear that they will leave tomorrow when we leave. Tika arrived, bringing with him a flute—a beautiful Nepali wooden instrument, the *lumu*; and, at nightfall gave us a small concert of folk tunes. Even Pasang tried her hand at playing a few notes. Whenever Mingma hears music of which she is familiar, she dances. With the dancing and the music, a beautiful evening was spent in Sengma—the music to be remembered during our trip.

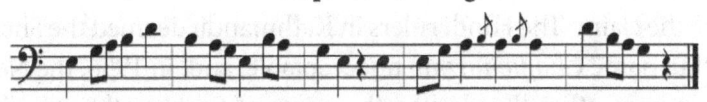

Lu
Nepali Folksong

As played by Tika on his *lumu*, a wooden Nepali flute.
This is a simple tune, performed in a melismatic manner,
adding several notes to one note, or syllable of text.

EVEREST
chumolungma चुमोलुन्ग्मा

Mount Everest, the world's tallest peak, sits on the border of Nepal and Tibet. In 2020, Nepal and China agreed on the new height of this peak as 8,848 meters or 29,031.7 feet. Today, along with the name of Mt. Everest given to the mountain by a British survey team led by Sir George Everest in 1852, it takes the Tibetan name of *Chomolungma*, "Goddess Mother of the World," first shown with this name on French geographer and cartographer D'Anville's 1733 Asian atlas. As countries have every right to name their landmarks (including renaming them as the United States did in 2015 with Mt. McKinley back to the original Athabaskan name of *Denali*, Nepal has also made the claim. The Hindi rulers in Kathmandu deemed the Sherpa/Tibetan name *Chomolungma* unacceptable; and, in 1956, the Nepali government officially adopted the name of *Sagarmatha*, translated as "the Head of the Earth touching the Heaven."[22] *Miyloangsangma* is the Tibetan/Buddhist goddess, the "Goddess of the Sky" who lives at the top of of Chomolungma; her virtue is Inexhaustible Giving. It is said that Tenzing Norgay followed her up Everest, and that she allowed him to be the first to summit Everest.[23]

---

22 Arnette, Alan, "What's in a name: Everest, Chomolungma, Sagamarmatha?" 2020, https://www.alanarnette.com/blog/2020/12/14/whats-in-a-name-everest-chomolungma-sagarmatha/.
23 "Miyolangsangma," 2022, https://en.wikipedia.org/wiki/Miyolangsangma.

We begin the hike late morning on a relatively sunny day; puffy, white, floating clouds are high in the sky. Before we leave, Phuti prepares the altar with juniper incense, after which she throws the incense with a bit of water, directly into the fire on the hearth. As I have never seen her use the incense in this manner (usually only in the morning, in front of a window), I wonder if the addition of water and fire is for luck. Phuti insists on carrying my backpack; and I, knowing that my hiking skills were still debatable, decided not to argue. Phuti said, as usual, "Phuti's pack." Even though we are going to be on this trip for six days, I can't remember Phuti packing anything of her own. Perhaps she slipped a few items into my backpack. Tika, in a sweet and gracious move, gave me a walking stick to help on the hike—one that he had made from a long branch. I kept this stick with me for the next two months, and I am sure it saved me many, many times. We said good-bye and set off.

Crossing the lower stream using the bridge I had tended for a month (I do not think Phuti noticed my engineering feat for there was nary an approving glance—she just walked across, no problem), I follow her down the ravine, past my earlier effort in climbing the ridge, to a much easier climb up and over the top. There are actual quasi-steps worn into the side of the cliff. Such irony--there must be a lesson in here somewhere. An extremely well-worn trail is at the top of the ridge, unlike the path I had discovered only days before. I try to keep Phuti's pace as she is really moving along; at this rate, we will get to Namche in no time. We walk steadily but quickly, now having joined with the path less traveled.

There is a synchronicity moment soon after we cross the bridge into Ghat. I am sitting on a bench outside a teahouse; and, shortly after, who should sit down to rest but two hikers from Colorado—a lovely couple on the Board of 'Bravo Colorado' in Vail, an important classical music festival in the summer. Phuti had disappeared into the teahouse, giving me a moment to chat with my newly found friends. After the fact, I wrote in my journal that they had many tales to relate about the festival (it is probably right that I do not remember any of those narratives). They moved on ahead, and I joined Phuti for a cup of tea. Looking back over the trek, Phuti seemed to know everyone that owned a teahouse on this trail; indeed, stopping at quite a few, many cups of tea were imbibed. In so doing, I was able to experience the many forms of the Khumbu outhouse that one could conceivably imagine. In Ghat, as we were about to leave, I looked back on the trail. I could see Sengma—so far away, sitting on the side of a mountain. Remembering my fixation on crossing the stream, I was astonished that it had taken me only a month to conquer this distance.

The path leading out of Ghat is narrow and extremely rocky, causing me to take care with every step. For the most part, we keep pace with the other hikers ahead. A column of long-eared donkeys, all carrying supplies and with bells attached on their harnesses, pass us by; the bells are ringing with every step they take—a cacophony of sound with a multitude of pitches and sounds. Every so often the animals allow us to pass, especially at the wider sections of the trail. Being behind the donkeys on the dirt paths is difficult; their hooves kick up mud and dust, making it hard to breathe. The trails differ from being simply packed dirt, or dirt with rocks, or in a town such as Ghat, surfaced with large, flat paver stones. As the hills are to our right, there are often high stone walls—I imagine preventing any slides. Unless a building or a small wall exists to our left, the valley is straight down a couple of thousand feet, the side of the path only identified with shrubs or scrub trees or just a rock or two. It is difficult not to stop for a few minutes to look at the scenery for now we are coming directly into the mountains. The views up ahead are astonishing with the white peaks showing their heads above the shorter summits. Phuti carries on, not stopping to stare as I would like. I dutifully follow. It is a beautiful day with blue skies above.

A porter passes by, strapped onto his back and around his head the most insane amount of Coca-Cola boxes—all totaled, they tower five feet over his head and to the sides. I cannot imagine the weight he is carrying. He actually had the breath to stop his momentum, chatting with Phuti for a minute. As we turn a corner, Kusum Kangaru comes into view. This mountain, seen in the distance from Sengma, is the mountain with my meditation waterfall. Up close, it looks so much higher than 6,300 meters. I have never seen mountains of this height—those that almost look as if they are touching the sky. A huge boulder (a *mani* stone) comes into view. The size of a large shed, it is covered with Tibetan writing, the familiar writing in white completely encasing the stone: "*Om mani padme hum.*" I am reminded that this *mantra*, if chanted with intention will bring peace and positive energy into the body. Soon after, we pass an even larger boulder with the same *mantra*, this one surrounded by hundreds of smaller, flat *mani* stones.

Another row of donkeys moves swiftly by—their bells clanking into the distance. Every so often we pass other little settlements with stone buildings decorated with blue or green window framings and doors. Each small village has a few homes, a couple of shops, and the occasional tea house. We pass a group of men chiseling stones for the construction of a building—the 'chink' of the hammers against the rock creating a rhythm of sorts. Phuti doesn't say very much other than being directional or giving a descriptive word about the village or mountain passed; and, as there are not hordes of hikers and animals on the trail, other than the bells and the voices of the accompanying porters, the hike is very peaceful. The occasional waterfall, a small *stupa*, *mani* stones, prayer wheels that we immediately turn, and stacked stones or cairns (the latter probably for good luck and assuredly of religious significance), all remind me of the culture and tradition that surrounds us as we make our way forward. We have been walking for quite a few hours; and an almost smooth stone path takes us into the village of Phakding—our goal for the first day's walk. We are met by rows of Buddhist prayer flags covering a wooden wall, and colorful homes and businesses line the path. A blue house sits on the hill among other stone and stuccoed constructions, and along with a Buddhist flagpole, welcomes us to the village. We will stay at a local tea house, the Mero Lodge, a popular resting stop for trekkers on the route. Our timing is impeccable as it begins to rain.

During this hike I have been walking behind Phuti the entire time. She has a constant walking rhythm—saying, or motioning very little, her tempo undeviating and fairly non-stop. When given a choice on dirt or stone stairs that are ascending, to either step directly on the stairs or walk on the side, Phuti usually takes the side option. Another Phuti tip: she often has one hand on her hip while walking, something I am trying in imitation. My feeling is that this practice supports the back/hip when going a long distance or up vertical climbs. I notice that I stand straighter with the hand on the hip—a tip that seems helpful. This hike seems more intense than my usual efforts because switchbacks are seen rarely, if at all, on the trail. These zigzags do cause a route to be longer but are much easier on the legs. Today, even though there are many downslopes, we have been gradually climbing, the path continually straightforward. I am thankful that since arriving on the eastern side of the valley, Phuti has been taking her time and walking at a moderate speed, but constantly.

The teahouse is quite comfortable with separate sleeping rooms to the side of the main living space and kitchen. My assigned room has a real bed, albeit with an extremely thin and, unfortunately, a hard mattress. No matter, it will be good to relax tonight. *Dal bhat* is the order of the evening—quite good, although not as *picante* or spicy, as the *dal bhat* in Phuti's kitchen. Men are sitting at the tables (perhaps guides or porters), along with a few young foreigners (German speaking)—all likely on a trek. Again, Phuti not only knows the gentleman who runs the teahouse but a few of the other gentlemen. As the hours turn to evening, something that I had not experienced for a month brightened the space: LIGHTS! There are electric lights! Taking the advantage to read in bed, I said goodnight, scrambled into my sleeping bag, and pulled out the Dumas book. I am almost at the end, so I must find another book during this trek. The atmosphere as I read is warm in terms of temperature as well as in the communion of those talking in the room next door. The sound of the river, far down in the valley, lulls me to sleep.

Phuti and I, after some toast and tea, leave Phakding in the morning under bright blue skies. Namche is our goal for today. An earthy smell is in the air after a brief rain shower last night. The evening was one of sleep-deprivation due to the constant rumbling of the Dudh Kosi. The river, moving south from its origination in the glacier area of Everest, becomes rapid and ferocious as the melting snow and ice moves downward. Even though in directional opposition, the river will be guiding us to Namche, being crossed several times during the trek. Almost immediately after leaving Phakding, we come to our first suspension bridge that is not too horrifyingly high. Buddhist flags are draped on the metal sides along with the white scarves of welcome, all signifying a safe journey. Unfortunately, Phuti points out a similar metal bridge a bit under us that had collapsed in the past, now hanging on to the opposite side of the river by a single cable. I must always remember to look straight ahead when we are crossing this river—in the class system of white-water rafting, at least a level IV or V. Definitely do not look down. Phuti tells me that we will cross two more of these suspension bridges before Namche; these are "much, much higher, and longer." Again—sharing too much information, and words always spoken with the most placid and serious of demeanors.

Across the river is quite a large village, Rimijung. We are met by a crowing, colorful rooster on a tin roof, alongside a large, polychromatic prayer wheel set into a stone wall. Taking the time to stop for a few minutes to turn the wheel, I run into two, young Americans from Detroit. On this trek I will certainly get my fill of speaking English and speechifying about Sengma, the cello and Bach. I am making up for last month's lost language. The two fellows move ahead, and we follow a row of very slow, burdened yuk-yaks; in turn, they are quickly passed by a column of fast-paced, rather sad-looking donkeys, all carrying loads of equipment and being led by porters. We pass the animals; it is never wise to be behind any of these creatures, lovable though they may be.

Leaving Rimijung, as we are now on the western side of the river, the scenery has changed. We turn a corner—what a view!

The mountains to our east, so distant in Sengma, are now almost capable of being touched. The paths are dirt and stone, high rocks on the left and straight down to the river on the right. I am, notwithstanding, spending a great deal of time looking down, in this instance to watch my step. According to my map, we should be crossing the river again on the way to the village of Monju, the gateway to the National Park, Sagarmatha. The column of donkeys come up from behind, their bells announcing our approach to another suspension bridge. As Phuti has predicted, this one is decidedly higher. We give the green light to the donkeys, conceding to their crossover in front of us. This bridge is longer than the first; the valley must be widening at this point. The bridge is also quite narrow, but hikers and porters coming towards us can pass as Phuti and I navigate our way over the clamor of the river.

A short hike and steps downward to Monju, bring us to the park entrance. A large wooden entryway in the design of a lofty open door, carved and covered with colorful symbols and signs with an inner iron gate, is open to all hikers. We need permits to enter the park; and, as always, Phuti is in charge, receiving two certificates from an officious looking gentleman at the entrance. As we move through the majestic doorway, large boulders with the familiar *mantra*, "om mani padme hum," written in white, greet us. "According to the Dalai Lama... *Om Mani Padme Hum* means that on the path of life, with intention and wisdom, we can achieve the pure body, speech and mind of a Buddha."[24] Surrounding us is a landscape photographer's dream—every mountainous shot is framed with the greenness of the valley. High walls, with the *mani* inscription covering the length and breadth of the stone, follow us as we maneuver down the rocky, cobblestone path. Next on the well-worn trail is the village of Jorsale, a resting spot for many before the short (so they say) but intense climb up to Namche.

---

24 Stewart-Brown, Charlie, "The Tibetan Buddhist Translation of Om Mani Padme Hum," 2022, https://indivyoga.com/the-meaning-of-om-mani-padme-hum-in-tibetan-buddhism/

In Jorsale, we stop at a lovely, small teahouse for a break. It is quite cold now as the wind has picked up; the little fire burning stove in the middle of the dining space is warming us as we sit with our tea. Skeptical that Phuti needs any preparation whatsoever, I mentally make ready for the steep climb of about 2,000 feet to Namche. Before leaving Jorsale, I see yaks for the first time. These animals have a huge frame, with short legs, long curved horns, and a quasi-humped back with long fur hanging down past the midpoint of their body. They are all loaded with cargo, ready to carry supplies up to the village.

And we are off! Waterfalls tumbling out of the mountain sides are in every nook and cranny, this emerging landscape leading us to the last metal suspension bridge before the climb. This last bridge is known as Hillary's Bridge, the skyway spanning the valley. The overpass, named after Sir Edmond Hillary, is insanely high and very long, almost 500 feet. As I cannot resist, I look down; the valley plunges many meters into the river. Decorated with colorful prayer flags and *khada*, the Buddhist white shawl, the bridge seems even lengthier due to what is beneath. Before we cross, we are asked to wait as the bridge has become too compromised with the weight of hikers and a group of yaks. As we walk across, the metal floor seems to bounce and sway, no doubt due to the high-altitude wind. Even the weight of the three or four yaks beginning the crossover, does not grant stability. The view is spectacular, but I was grateful when we finally crossed onto earth. This bridge is definitely not for the faint of heart.

The hike up to Namche begins. I gingerly walk along an extremely rocky path; at times it doesn't really look like a path at all—only rocks and boulders strewn about. I think back to the first expedition of Hillary and Tenzing Norgay in 1953. Their attempt was from the south; we must be following in their footsteps as we make our way on this rocky trail. Another porter goes by with a ridiculous amount of freight on his back. Evidently, these porters get a very small amount of money for their labor. Phuti tells me they make the equivalent of $1 a kilo to carry supplies from Lukla to Namche; and, for that amount, they accomplish the eight to ten hours walk in one day. Every porter that we meet (Phuti engages each one in conversation) is smiling—happy and proud that he is doing this work to provide for his family. As we tread along, the path is becoming more reasonable—packed dirt. We are going slowly, following a group of yaks with their handlers. I am thankful for the animals, even with the dust, for their slow speed. They are leading the pace for those behind. I have no desire to hasten our momentum up the steep path. The surrounding terrain is one of a forest; pine and fir trees border the dusty trail. At one point, Phuti pointed out the national bird of Nepal, the Himalayan Monal, recognized by its iridescent blue and orange plumage.

The trail (I am convinced it maintains a 45° angle) continues for another hour or so. Due to our slow and steady speed, I find the climb is within the bounds of possibility. Finally, we come to the uphill basin that is Namche Bazar known to all as the 'Gateway to Everest.' The rather large village is on the edge of the mountain we just climbed, saddled high on the hill. The possibility of the entire village sliding off the mountain seems very real. The fact that it has been here for centuries belies that probability. The village is surrounded by tall green mountains; behind those, even higher snow-covered peaks look down over the area.

The stone houses with green-framed windows, are set on the hill, noticeably on terraced levels; and as all Sherpa homes (and businesses) for the most part, they are arranged with their backs to the hill, windows facing the sun. This is a rough terrain with dirt streets and walkways, a challenging environment. Even the surrounding high peaks in their majestic beauty auger trouble, perhaps because of what we know about the danger that exists. My outsider knowledge of the Sherpa people has shown me that their amicable nature in working with those in the climbing industry enable them to exist in this rugged but beautiful land. After stopping for a moment at our hotel, the Galaxy ($4/night with unlimited amounts of tea), I leave Phuti and begin to explore. It is mid-afternoon, so I have an hour or two before supper. I have one major item on my mind—to find an email service.

From the hotel, I am led upward along narrow streets laid with smooth stone pavers and with steps marking the way. Coming to an open space, I look back to see a curved basin filled with homes and shops from bottom to top—an incredible sight. The market area is reminiscent of the Thamel area of Kathmandu except on a slant. Shops are lining the street with clothes for sale hanging from the front; and signs are advertising exchange, bars, a pizzeria, hotels, trekking supplies, mountain equipment—anything a climber might need. Then, turning a corner, I see a sign with the words, 'Cyber Café.' It is hard to believe, but it has taken me a day and a half of walking to find an internet and phone service. It is a small stone building attached to others in various shapes of disrepair. Along with yet another cup of tea, I send a few emails and make a phone call to my son. Jamie had no idea where or how I was, not having heard from me in over a month. Suddenly, life has taken on new meaning—a cliché, but at this moment in time, so true.

In Namche, the shopper's (hiker's) paradise, the expectation is to bargain, the technique of which I quickly learn. I buy a few trinkets to take home, a scarf for Phuti, and a sweet bun at the bakery before heading back to the hotel. Unfortunately, there are no private rooms at the Galaxy; the only sleeping accommodations are on the benches in the main room. At supper (a spicy *dal bhat* with green vegetables), I meet a group of five men from Kansas including two sets of dads and sons, two of whom are quite ill. Thinking to myself that I have remained healthy up to now, I speak too soon for the evening transforms into my watershed moment— that I am not above being ill. I manage to sleep amid the chatter after feeling quite badly. I discover that there is a limit to the amount of rice one can consume.

Phuti tells me that the early morning is the time to view Everest—the time when the weather will probably be clear. If we climb above Namche for about an hour, there is evidently the perfect spot for seeing the panorama—the place known to all as the Viewpoint. Climbing to this location will entail a hike of an increase in elevation to 13,000 feet, another 400 meters. With that in mind, we begin the hike to the top of the ridge above Namche at 5:00 in the morning. I am feeling good and excited to climb; and furthermore, the sky is clear—not a cloud in sight. It is cold, however; Phuti and I have on our warm jackets. The climb from Namche is steadily upwards on a steep, rough, rocky trail with stone steps adding to the difficulty (Phuti is walking on the side; it looks too slippery for me). Trekkers use this hike from Namche to the Viewpoint and to a hotel, the Everest View, for acclimatization purposes. For trekkers going on to Everest, there is a saying, "hike high, sleep low." For example, they will hike up to the hotel, then return to sleep at Namche. At certain places, the trail is very narrow, one side heading straight down to the river which appears to be a mere stream far down in the valley. After an hour, the path becomes quite bare, a fairly flat surface with low green shrubs on either side. This is a massive hill, the only sound being early morning birds, and, surprisingly for this early, a helicopter flying over to the landing strip above Namche, in Syampoche.

We round a corner and Phuti points— 'there'. The panorama of the Everest massif (Everest, Lhotse and Nuptse) with Ama Dablam to the east, is before us and completely unobstructed. I am staring at the DaVinci of landscapes. MOUNT EVEREST! Astounding! I could see the Hillary Step on Everest; and, at one point, I could see a slight avalanche cascading down Lhotse. There is still not a cloud in the early morning sky although the wind has picked up, and it is quite chilly. We are joined by quite a few hikers; groups from Colorado and Montana and some Germans from the Phakding lodge. I am elated, almost euphoric, to share this moment with everyone.

As it is almost 8:00, I decide to treat Phuti to breakfast at the Everest View. Another 15 minutes along a northern path, and we arrive at the hotel. On the terrace outside, we sit in silence over a pot of coffee and an egg sandwich, the silence generated because of the panorama of Everest before us, along with blue skies above and wisps of clouds in the valley far below. It is difficult to describe the scale of the terrain as we are above the clouds; the Dudh Kosi thousands of feet below creating not one iota of sound. I take one minute to ponder this hotel. It is an expensive lodge built by the Japanese, seemingly to serve only the wealthy. Phuti is harsh but honest, describing the "lazy, rich foreigners" who fly by helicopter to the nearby airport in Syampoche (instead of Lukla) to shorten their hike. Much like the commercial aspects of climbing these high mountains, they miss the intensity of the struggle, of the energy and hard work necessary to reach a vantage point such as this one. So much is lost.

The love I have of Everest and the well-known climbing mountains is because of the mystery. I appreciate the desire to climb; and for various reasons, the climbers needing to depend upon others (in the case of Everest, the Sherpas) to meet their challenge. It is quite wondrous that a person can look at climbing a mountain, and yet with the mountain's many risks decides to take on the challenge alone—only depending upon themselves, their intelligence and ability. The Eiger, Everest, and so many others—these silent monuments beckon to the warriors.

Reinhold Messner, an Italian mountaineer who made the first solo ascent of Mount Everest in 1980, speaks of the evolution of the climbing industry today. In his book, *Everest, Expedition to the Ultimate*, he speaks of the 'consumable' Everest:

"Since the beginning of the 1990s more than a thousand people a year converge on the flanks of the world's highest mountain: hundreds on the north side (Tibet), with the bulk continuing to approach from the south (Nepal). Although permits have become more expensive and parties are threatened with all sorts of restrictions, Mount Everest has degenerated into a 'fashionable' mountain. Dozens make it to the summit each year. The increase in numbers attempting the climb produces a correspondingly higher number of successes and, on top of that, with so many expeditions on the mountain simultaneously, the actual climbing has become far easier: the ice fall is protected with fixed ropes and ladders, the trail broken and marked, high camps established, so that the line of the route is obvious for most of the way to the summit. Today's Everest climber is scarcely ever exposed or completely alone; he or she climbs in a crocodile formation. And any exceptions to this scenario are increasingly rare."[25]

Being able to sit for a time to watch a mountain such as Everest is enough for me. It is my own 'climb.' It is my hope that in my journey with Bach, I can also state as did Messner, "I wanted to climb high again in order to be able to see deep inside myself."[26]

Phuti decides to return to Namche. Energized from the rest, I follow the path north for a while, unbelieving of the mountains surrounding me. Meeting a young fellow on the trail just standing in complete ecstasy, not believing he was there, I realized that I had found a true compatriot. There is so much that could be said about Namche and Mount Everest, but this will have to do. The height is so extreme—a topsy-turvy world. I can see Ama Dablam, an incredible mountain dominating the view to the eastern side of the river. Although not as tall as Everest at a little over 22,000 feet, the mountain is evidently a difficult, complicated climb due to ice and rock. If I kept going, in another eight or ten days I would be at the South Base Camp (almost 23 miles). It takes more time than I would think due to the elevation difference and needed acclimatization rest days. For me, this morning's hike was sufficient.

I return to Namche, no longer in the dark of early morning but in the bright sunlight. I look downward to my left, past the scrub and the rocks, to see the land swooping down to the river where the perspective of the vertical depth alongside the vertical height is difficult to comprehend. Another helicopter flies over. Thinking of those on board, I realize that with my feet solidly on a ground that I have trod for two days, I am the most grateful person in the world to have not bypassed life.

The next day, as Phuti wants to stay in the village, I decide to hike alone up to Khumjung, two kilometers above Namche (almost a two-hour climb), to see the monastery and to see the school built

---

25   Messner, Reinhold, *Everest, Expedition to the Ultimate*, The Mountaineers, 1999, 1.
26   Messner, Reinhold, *Everest, Expedition to the Ultimate*, ii.

by Edmund Hillary in 1961. Today—Khumjung; tomorrow we will head home. Having sunny skies for two days now, there was not a drop of rain last night for the first time: great climbing weather.

Leaving Namche, I am taking a different route (more north) than the one taken yesterday, although the height difference is much the same—up to 12,500 feet. This direction takes me on yet another steep climb—more rocky paths and many precipitous steps. Climbing ever higher, the view of Namche becomes a concave village in miniature. Following a group of yaks and porters, I am led to a sign pointing to Khumjung-Khunde, Khunde being another small village set alongside its neighbor, Khumjung. Khunde has the only hospital in the area, the medical clinic also developed by Hillary (Pasang's deep cut comes to mind). Tika's stick clicks on the stone; the only other sounds being the yak bells and the thump of the animal's hooves. Without a complaint gaining voice, I realize that I am adapting to climbing. When the direction is consistently up, ascension becomes quite normal and familiar.

As I arrive at the top of the ridge, I cross the airport at Syampoche. As a matter of fact, the term 'airport' is not reasonable in this instance. There is not a soul in sight. No one is waiting for a lift; a couple of helicopters sit silently. Large containers and bundles have been deposited in a small roped-off area—all on a large, scraggly green and partly dirt field. The airport, along with dropping off Phuti's 'lazy foreigners,' is used primarily for bringing in supplies for medical emergencies; therefore, I have a suspicion that little more in terms of ground support is needed. A lone crow's husky, squawking caw is the only sound in the wind.

The trail takes me through a path surrounded by fir trees, an unlikely sight at this elevation. I am approaching Khumjung, the village sitting at the foot of the holy Sherpa mountain of Khumbila, 'God of Khumbu.' Mount Khumbila at almost 19,000 feet is so respected that no one is allowed to climb the mountain. The prayer flags on bamboo poles that line the steps into the village are to honor Khumbila. From this standpoint, looking down at Khumjung with its coordinated green rooftops, the stone walls of loose rocks piled on top of each other separating fields from homes—all present an orderly impression of this small village. The vista is a commanding spectacle with the view of Ama Dablam and Kang Taiga in the east (both at almost 22,400 feet), and the Rowaling mountains in the west (consisting of more than 20 peaks above 6,000 meters).[27] Once again, I am like the gentleman in ecstasy—there are moments in life when one sees the world in a different light and in complete awe. This was one of them.

Khumjung is considered a remote area village with a small monastery and the Hillary School. After taking the steps downward into the village, I am met by a huge white *chorten* and rows of *mani* stones with their white inscriptions piled on top of a long wall. I pass the stone school with a ribbed tin roof, first built by the famous climber for young Sherpa children. Seeing a few older kids playing ball in the playing field, I ponder Mingma and Pasang and their seemingly erratic education. Granted, since my initial walk from Lukla over the now-destroyed Dudh Kosi bridge, a three-hour walk one way would be required for the girls to attend the school in Chaurikharka (another Hillary school). If only another bridge could be built.

Walking through the narrow paths of the village, the sights are many: piles of yak dung used at this elevation for burning in the fireplaces are curing on the sides of the houses; clothes are drying on the walls; and people are hoeing the fields, these fields separated by the extremely organized stone walls. I come to two large white *chortens* with golden steeples and rows of prayer wheels. The rolling sound as I revolve the spheres combine with the sounds of Khumjung: bells hanging from the necks of yaks leaving for Namche, the laughter of children playing in the dusty yards (one young boy flying a kite in the wind), and the light whisper of workers in the fields—a placid and untroubled scene.

Advertised as being in the monastery, a 300-year-old yeti scalp will have to be seen another day. Unfortunately, the building

---

27 "Peaks of Rowaling," Highland Expeditions, https://highlandexpeditions.com/peaks-of-rolwaling/.

is closed momentarily. The scalp, according to a gentleman at the Galaxy, did undergo some examination and was found to be fashioned from the hide of an animal, probably a goat-antelope native to Himalayas. The monastery, quite beautiful from the outside, is the center of Sherpa culture and religion in Khumjung.

Almost noon, it is time to retrace my steps back to Namche for lunch. A little over an hour, and I am back. Going down is so painless! Wandering around the narrow, crowded streets of Namche where the only direction is either steeply up or steeply down, the sounds are creating a noisy chaos. In the busy marketplace, people are enthusiastically talking, water is running, the bells of the donkeys chime along with the birds in the wind, and the 'chinking' sound of construction is constant. Market sellers from Tibet are recognizable by a long braid and red headpieces. Their colorful rugs and smaller mats are draped over the stone walls while their yaks stand silently by. The Namche vendors seem to have every consumable known to man laid out on tarps or plastic sheeting—for the most part, huge cuts of meat (not sure of the animal) and many known and unknown vegetables. A large white chorten with its all-seeing eyes and a golden steeple stands outside the entrance gate to Namche, surrounded by prayer flags and underneath, at least 100 prayer wheels. Walking around the chorten square, I managed to turn each wheel, sending prayers into the wind.

As the monsoons are beginning to diminish, I get the feeling that this is real climbing weather. I hear that there is a Spanish group that has been at the Everest Base Camp for quite some time, preparing to climb when the weather allows. I wonder how they are faring and if safe.

We are staying tonight in a different tea house, the Nimu Guest House; regrettably, the sleeping arrangements remain the same—on benches and, as in Sengma, in the main living space. We are planning to leave Namche in the early afternoon tomorrow, reversing our previous schedule and staying overnight in Phakding once again. Over dinner (very spicy fried potatoes and vegetables), the Nimu owner talked about the yetis, saying that they lived 100 years ago and added, "Now is not the time—they were high in the mountains."

Realizing that the saying, 'one doesn't miss what one can't have' is foolish for I miss eating a 'real' breakfast—the benefit of having toast and tea every morning (eggs were a pleasant diversion) has run its course. I suggest to Phuti that we undertake another climb. Being mobile on an upward slant, especially when the result is another view of Everest along with refreshments, is my new activity. Hiking to the Everest View Lodge again, Phuti and I have a very special brunch—a version of French toast and syrup, reminding me of an American breakfast at an old-fashioned diner. I sit on the rock ledge with my back to Everest while Phuti takes a photo of me against this background—a final and breathtaking view of this peak. The two hikers from Colorado (we met in Ghat) pass us once again as we return to our lodge. The trail and gateway to the Khumbu area is so compact that it is not unusual to run into others who are banding together in the adventure. The 'Bravo Colorado' crew, promising to leave unwanted books in Ghat on their return to Lukla, are going on to Tengboche—a beautiful monastery on the other side of the river and higher in elevation. I am disappointed that we have decided not to cross the river from Namche, but it is time to go home.

Returning to the guest house, Phuti discovers that Chongba came to Namche with a trekking group and has already left; we missed him by about 30 minutes. Phuti would like to stay another day; however, I am somewhat tired of trying to sleep in semi-dark, dreary Sherpa kitchens while everyone chats. Phuti is kind enough to agree to head home. I feel a need to return to Sengma and Bach. As we make our way down Namche's steep path to the Hilary Bridge and seeing glimpses of Everest at points on the trail, I contemplate the mountain and its power and energy. I remember those who have, with incredible endurance and willpower, survived the magnetism of this highest peak. Sadly, I think of those who did not survive their efforts and did not have the opportunity to take this path home. In quick time, in less than two hours, we come down Namche's massive cliff. I am thankful.

We make record time in returning. I should have kept track of the number of bridges crisscrossing the Dudh Kosi—not only the number, but the type. Every bridge compelled me to become un-Buddha-like, as in, "please, Buddha, let this bridge last for ONE more person." After lunch in Jorsale, the hike is going so well we almost decide that Sengma is within reach. As it looks as if it might rain (my pack on Phuti's shoulders is also quite heavy—we bought too much in Namche), we stop again in Phakding at the Mero Lodge, deciding to head home tomorrow. The overnight break in our journey becomes one of a festive celebration for all we have seen in the past few days. A very charming young fellow, perhaps 16 or 17, began to play Nepali folk songs on the *seranji* after our dinner. For this evening, a private room was not necessary; I was amenable to a bench near the evocative sound of the music. The next morning, we head towards Ghat and home.

A word about the past few days: to be honest, devising this journey was a bit of a lark—an adventure, an escapade. Not that I was **not** serious for I had a definable purpose—Bach. But for me to go to Nepal by myself to live in the Himalayas—the idea was an adventure of the first order. The actuality of what I have just seen in the mid-point of my life in Khumbu has been a bit of a jolt. I am not sure that I knew what really could be accomplished when creating the plan. The 'escapade' has turned into something bordering upon transcendency. I have discovered that I can make something happen that has the capability of changing my life. Is it possible that an experience such as this be the one that sets the stage for what is next—this preparation for death that is such a large part of the Buddhist tradition? I do not know, for these are just words, but I believe that now I know the possibility exists. Remembering this entire experience as something extraordinary is an understatement.

I will be returning to the rather dreary sameness of every day and the silence, real and imaginary, that accompanies this monotony; and yet, Bach is there to keep me steady—to give me a reason to keep putting one foot in front of the other. Looking for more in my exploration of the suites, I am hoping that my experience with Everest (and I did call it 'transcendent') will permeate every note and phrase I play. This will be an internal triumph, one I may not fully realize, if ever. Even so, the attempt to discover in Bach the true meaning of the words that for 300 years have been spoken in the same breath as his name: hypnotic power, divine order, tranquility—these are the same words I use when speaking of Everest, Eiger, DaVinci—perfect examples of art, both in nature and man-made. Put simply, in planning this journey with Bach, I wanted to believe that relearning his music in the highest mountains of the world with the surrounding religious traditions, I could discover a new way, a new interpretation of the Suites that in turn I could offer to my students. I do not think I will ever know, for sure, if I was successful.

Another jolt to reality: we are now back in Sengma, October 12. The girls have survived and are quite happy to see us. It being late afternoon, Tika will leave in the morning. A wash-up in the trusty basin, and physically, I am feeling quite normal again.

It rains during the evening. Now I know we're back. Surprisingly, after missing Chongba in Namche, he has arrived home with his trekking group—two porters and two Europeans from Salzburg, Sepp and Edith. The Austrians are an interesting, English-speaking couple who had refrained from climbing but had enjoyed hiking in the area. Because the people of Khumbu lack so much that we take for granted, they often travel to Nepal bringing clothes, medicines, and toys to the Sherpas each time they visit. As they are choosing to stay in their tents outside even with the rainy weather (they will be leaving in the morning), I am feeling a bit guilty for I am in my little room, snug in my sleeping bag.

For the past week, I had thought little about the coming month in Sengma, my mind being preoccupied with the trek and the terrain. Now, I am free to renew my worries about probable difficulties in leaving for Nagarkot in mid-November. As Chongba is returning to Lukla soon, I ask if he can arrange my return plane ticket to Kathmandu. I realize that I am over-planning—that all will happen in due course. Thinking about the people in Lukla waiting for their flights on these tiny planes and waving their tickets in the face of the frustrated boarding official, these thoughts do not help a sense of tranquility. My original tickets, now useless, were made for December 1, directly from Lukla to Kathmandu and back to the States. Making these plans in Boulder was a cinch—in Nepal, challenging. As to the 'how' and the 'when,' everything is a struggle. Chongba's, "all will be ok," is encouraging on a certain level. A small comfort is knowing that Tshering will return to help in the travel back to Kathmandu and onward to Nagarkot.

I have returned to playing Bach every morning, enjoying the fact that I can literally run through suites I-III and sections of IV. My fingers must also understand that returning to the fluidity they had achieved before we left for Namche is a priority. It is amazing what a few days of not practicing will do to the flexibility, not to mention the necessary calluses which are not aided with all this humidity. I wish for as much sun and warmth as possible as I enter the last month in Khumbu.

Suite IV in Eb Major—the key, like the C Major, has a feeling of great determination. The feeling is one of purpose—of persistence and tenaciousness. I realize that I am speaking of those who are climbing in the mountains as I sit with the cello, thinking about their struggle. I have been influenced by those I have met and everything I have seen; as a result, my inclination will be to bring out the inherent quality of determination in this suite—a quality I can produce with rhythmic energy and depth of sound. This suite is rather stern and solemn, mimicking my seriousness as I enter the next phase of my journey.

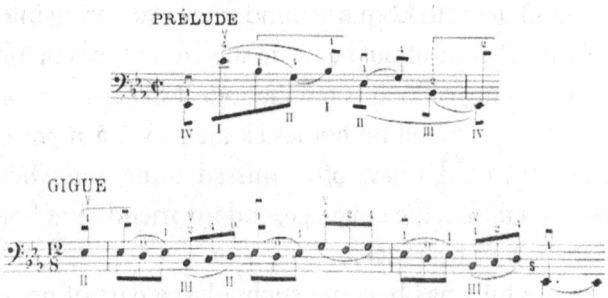

It is a complicated suite and like life, the work is constantly trying to extricate itself from its intricacies. As I am playing, the notes and phrases weave in and out, trying to find a resolution. The performance of this suite is unlike the climb of Everest, following the ropes and those leading the way. Everest could be Suite I, in G Major—taking the helicopter to Syampoche, joyfully taking the short route, and feeling good about life! Suite IV is comparable to Ama Dablam—ice inhibits the climber in finding the correct path, but when the path is clear, resolution is brief.

The temperatures of the mountains have drifted south. The cold of winter is beginning to settle in. I have the clothing (the long underwear is a constant); I only worry about the cello in the dryness and cold—an increasing problem. As an instrumentalist, I am always mindful of the wood cracking; these openings can be difficult to repair. Some cracks I could close with my clamps and glues; if too open or deep, I could not. Another analogy could be made with the crevasses in the glaciers, or is that taking my instrumental/Himalayan analogy too far?

A few days have passed since our return from the Everest trek. The sun is out today and the mountains in the distance have become clear and inviting. The practice on IV is coming along as I connect more with the key of Eb. It is hard to believe that the first four suites are finally feeling comfortable. V and VI are looming ahead, but it appears that this project may have a happy ending—the complex schedule has done its magic. A new book picked up in a tea house in Jorsale, 'Pope Joan' by Woolcroft (based on a ninth century legend) has been read. It is rather a good novel to keep my mind from wandering into anxious territory. I am not good about being 'in the present' except for the time I am sitting with my cello. It is fascinating, at my age (my birthday is tomorrow) that I can still be homesick after over a month. When I have been on the road, I have often missed home, and when abroad, the States —its culture, the language, and my friends; but I have never been melancholy or heartsick.

Hiking the hills has become such a large part of my existence in Sengma; and to walk under blue skies instead of making my way through cloudy skies, fog or rain, is a marvel. Some flowers are still in abundant bloom along the nearby stone walls. As the weather is so beautiful, playing the cello outside may be a nice change of pace. I find a tall wicker basket on the ground floor (upside down it is perfect for sitting), gather my cello and bow, and play a suite or two just outside the house. Facing the mountains, the feeling was one of sweeping gratification—a moment of tranquility. As I have decided to adhere to the original schedule involving moving out of the mountains in mid-November, I realize that there is appreciably more to accomplish before that time. Besides Bach, the entire experience in Khumbu is a memory that I must somehow etch into the part of the brain that stores these recollections.

The days go by in slow but determined succession. I really cannot tell a Sunday from a Thursday. No email arrived from our recent runner; consequently, I read old messages to keep connected. I can't seem to settle with the uniformity that fills every day; I feel as though I am always eager for something. I wonder what marks the difference for this Sherpa family. Every day is the same in length and in substance except for the occasional incident as reported by a neighbor or by Chongba when he is home: "Today another tiger took away a cow." (Evidently there is a real jungle up there.) Another 'happening' occurs when Tika arrives to work in the fields. Today, besides his radio set-up, he brought an old battery-powered tape player with cassettes of Nepali pop music. The popular songs sound ancient; nevertheless, I love the joy and freedom that comes from bringing relatable music into their home. As Mingma and Pasang always dance, Pasang devotedly following Mingma's free form movements, these occasions of coming together with music establish a fleeting, but most welcome, connection with me and with the family.

Tika has a joy about him, a feeling that I don't often see with the family as they seem so serious and, in general, placid. Mingma and Pasang must be completely comfortable with me now as they are truly trying my patience when I am playing (a favorite activity is literally taking my bow off the string). Or it could just be my practicing the Fifth Suite in C minor, this key being rather depressing; and the nature of these two little girls is anything but depressing. Along with the repetition that is necessary with memorizing, the girls are saying, "Stop, enough!" in their own way. The beginning of the fifth is heart-stopping with its announcement of looming disaster:

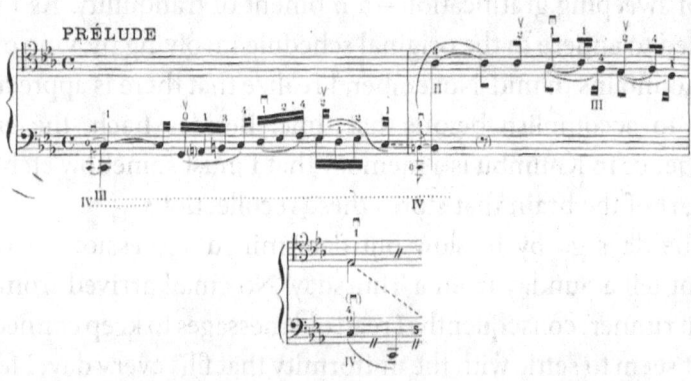

This suite, like the second suite, is melancholy; the key of C minor takes 'dark' to another level. The Prelude, not unlike an organ in a huge cathedral with all stops out, announces the approaching tragedy or catastrophe. With the lowest string of the instrument vibrating, the sound of the opening octave is similar to that of the *dungchen*, the Tibetan long horn to which I was introduced that first evening in Sengma at the death ceremony. The horn's haunting wail, at times imitating the sound of the wind, can be reproduced with my bow using the right combination of weight and speed (poetically, I can imagine the air blowing me to the highest peak). The Prelude, as does much of this suite, takes on the form of a Buddhist chant, chants themselves being similar to musical incantations. Even the melodic second gavotte (a French dance) is remarkably somber as an intense sadness takes over.

If there is a truthfulness to the parallelism of each suite with my disposition in Sengma, I must succumb to the feeling, knowing that all such episodes in life are temporary and fleeting. It is important to feel, and then to let go. Sadness is also often attributed to loss, and I believe in remembrance brings strength. This suite has an extraordinary Sarabande—heartfelt and sensuous. Yo-Yo Ma, cellist, has performed this movement for memorial services world-wide, for example, in Boston in remembrance of the Boston Marathon tragedy, and in Paris during Armistice Day. A more reflective and beautiful work has rarely been composed. For me, the Sarabande of Suite V is second only to Beethoven's Cavatina in his String Quartet, Op.130.

In terms of the big picture, the suites are going well—I-IV are memorized, and serious work is being accomplished on V and VI. My complicated schedule, concentrating on one suite while adding movements from the others each day, is serving me well. I must not forget, however, about my desire to explore the act of meditation in practicing. Focusing on the waterfall has produced results up to a point. I am coming to realize, however, that when I have spoken about the importance of focus in practicing to my young students, in being more 'present,' I have been asking the student to engage in a form of meditation. It has become clear during the time with my cello in Sengma and being open to the traditions surrounding me, that in the physicality of finding a solution to a technical or musical dilemma quickly and clearly, freeing my mind of outside thoughts or distractions, I am entering into meditation of a certain kind.

In these days of more sunshine, time is moving slowly. I can sit outside, enjoying the interaction of the Sherpas as they go about the daily cultivation of the croplands. Phuti spends many hours in the potato fields with other women from the houses nearby. The men not on treks are moving cattle, plowing fields, or hauling construction materials for repairs in Sengma or neighboring villages. In the middle of the afternoon, everything stops. Phuti comes in to boil potatoes over the fire, taking them out into the fields for everyone to enjoy. I spend too much time participating in this afternoon teatime; as a result, I may never eat another potato again! Mingma and Pasang sit with the other women as if they were already part of this older community. How I wish that I could communicate with them on a level other than games and single words, simply to find out what they are thinking. I feel as though I am missing out on an important part of this journey. I do not, however, want to interfere with the rhythm of the household; it is enough for me to observe and learn, knowing that much is beyond my comprehension. The family has given me so much; in this relatively short period of time, it is not necessary to fully fathom all.

I try to walk to the higher elevations of Sengma's mountain whenever possible (staying far away from the jungle). From the heights, looking north, I can see additional snow on the distant mountains (Kang Taiga, Tramserku) that we could almost touch a couple of weeks ago. To see the stars out in the evening three days in a row is strikingly new. The immensity of the sky (*girpo*—big) highlights the isolation in this small village in Khumbu. There is no doubt that this region is one of the best places to stargaze on this earth, located far from large cities and with its altitude, free of haze. If one is looking at Khumbu from afar, one would see extraordinary layers: mountains, then clouds, then mountains above the clouds, and then the stars. Sitting outside in the cold with not one electric light around, I contemplate the seeming simplicity and naturalness of the people that, perhaps, is a result of the sky above. *Miyolangsangma*, the Goddess of the Sky, whose virtue is 'inexhaustible giving,' has granted this virtue, through prayer, to those who have lived under her shadow for hundreds, for thousands of years.

I decide to go to Ghat for the books—for *kitab*, that were promised by my fellow trekkers in Namche. I encounter Peter (the Phakding trekker) half-way to the village. In leggings, shorts and a headband and looking trekking-worn, he is keeping his promise to visit us in Sengma—to see the Sherpa village that is hosting a cellist playing Bach. Turning around, I lead the way back to Sengma. It is the first visit with an American in the home I have shared for almost two months. The visit begins with a small stroll up and down the village paths. Tika is plowing the near-by fields with the yuk yaks, the cattle hitched to his homemade plow. I am constantly in awe of the tools he uses for work in the fields and the ingenuity it has taken to construct them. Taking a break, Tika decides that threshing would be the perfect activity for our newcomer. For me, the coordination needed to use the insane, hand-crafted threshing tool is still unattainable; however, Peter could have a new occupation as a Nepali thresher. It certainly looks more user-friendly than in reality—the swing must be aligned just so. Filled with laughter and good humor, the morning goes quickly by. A reaction to an environment that has been missing for some time, today I have involved myself in a life other than my own. I chose the solitude; I did not choose the loneliness that came from being isolated and yet surrounded by others.

In treading our way back to Ghat, Peter tells me about his adventure in the mountains. There had been a big storm while he was up north, laying down a meter of snow, preventing him from climbing Kala Patthar (over 18,500 feet), a peak in proximity to the Everest massif and is said to have been the original base camp for Everest. The amount of rain (and the resultant snow) has been extremely problematic for the climbers in the high mountains. Peter had heard about a tragedy on Mera Peak (over 21,000 feet) but did not know the details. It was later reported that on the 21st, a porter died, and a storm trapped more than nine or ten climbers for two days on the mountain. Heavy snow and whiteout conditions had caught the trekkers on their way down—some became lost. One person is still missing.[28] Tragedies happen, and yet the climbers will still vie for the top—"because it's there."[29]

Peter's interest in Buddhism is like mine; he has forever longed for a trek in the mountains of Khumbu for he knew that through the experience he would achieve a certain communion with the sacred as well as the secular. After an afternoon lunch with tea and a delicious noodle soup at Hamy's lodge, Peter began his hike to Lukla. Tomorrow, he catches his flight back to Kathmandu and eventually back to America and the UK. Having Peter spend the day in Sengma was a very special one indeed.

I asked, looked, and found no books—a depressing moment. Did the Americans fail to remember, or have they not yet returned to Ghat? Except for the Dalai Lama's book, I have only read two novels since arriving at Sengma. What I would sacrifice for an exceptional non-fiction! I have solely myself to blame as I could have carried the books with me from Namche. On the other hand, Phuti was carrying an already-hefty backpack and would have refused my overture to give assistance. Perhaps next weekend, the volumes will magically appear. I repeatedly ponder my original idea of the monastery in Tibet; how ludicrous that idea seems at the present, and how important is communication—physical, verbal, and written.

The hike to and from Ghat is beginning to feel routine. As there is only one path, with no switchbacks as it climbs up and over whatever lies ahead, there is no possibility of getting lost. I am incorporating Phuti's technique of the hand on the hip. It is interesting how the position does seem to help unless I am just drawing at straws to make the hike a little more psychologically comfortable. Today, a few macaques are on fence posts or in the

---

28   Benavides, Angela, "One Dead, One Missing on Mera Peak," 2021, https://explorersweb.com/one-dead-one-missing-on-mera-peak/.
29   "Because it's there," Forbes Magazine, October 2001. https://www.forbes.com/global/2001/1029/060.html?sh=32d47b4c2080

shrubbery lining the path along with a dog or two on a doorstep—all gathered to watch the sole hiker pass by. The home of the instrument maker, Luc-Dawa, is quiet—the door closed. That being the case, I continue, not pausing to exchange greetings. Arriving back in Sengma, I find Phuti collecting beans from the garden. A little assistance is always offered if she is hard at work; at the same time, I know her answer if I put forward the proposition—and yet, I offer anyway, only to be sternly rebuffed.

A moment in time often helps to differentiate one day from another. Our creator of musical instruments, Luc-Dawa, is in Sengma to make a bed for Phuti (I wonder where she will put it). As he will stay for two days, the bed will cost about 200 R a day (about $2.50) plus food. Using a combination of modern tools and old-fashioned methods, he is utilizing the notch system of putting two pieces of wood together—few nails are being used in total. He is also a gentleman imbued with the Sherpa patience with children whose temperaments I have yet to master; the two girls are scampering around on the bed, even while he is working. I consider this an example of the Sherpa and his inexhaustible virtue of giving—giving the goodness of patience.

Save for the one time I was ill in Namche, I have been unscathed in terms of illness, perpetually thankful for the small bottles of preventative medicine. I had a tick on my neck one evening; Phuti thankfully was able to remove the creature. Six weeks left before the journey home, and I venture that I will be able to prevail. Not least it seems as though the sun has appeared more often than not. Perhaps the monsoon weather of Khumbu is at its end; the climbers up north must be thankful.

Although I recognize that my life in Sengma is unquestionably an exploit to be remembered, I do not believe that the feeling of being sorry for myself has ever abated. I am tired of the experience—of just being, of the tedium, of the dark, of the extreme hiking, of the unknown, and, surprisingly, of the repetition of the food. As might be expected, I feel extreme guilt for complaining as I am indebted to this family and to Pemba for this adventure—perhaps even emerging as one of crucial significance in my future narrative. The undertaking is not one to be dismissed—a true dichotomy.

I complain about the sameness of the food; nevertheless, I add that Phuti, with only a pan or two and an open fire, makes a four-star Sherpa restaurant out of the most basic ingredients. That being said, potatoes sometimes three times a day and the almost twice-a-day *dal bhat*, is a bit much. Yesterday, I found a roach in my soup; and, as these little insects seem to be always scampering around the fire, I was not surprised at all. The unusual becomes the usual—a certain monotony unto itself. I have become very blasé about all thing's food oriented. Have I mentioned Phuti preparing food on the floor? Pasang just urinated in the same spot. Nonchalant I am.

The days at the end of October are proving to be beautiful and gloriously sunny. Today, two e-mails appeared from God knows where. They just materialized. Always loving the runner's visits, Dawa (usually) is a silent ghost. The news from home, although these messages being few and far between, is a definite break, another 'happening,' in the indistinguishability of one day from another. This constancy is defeating—is getting the better of me. After two months, I am concluding that the household is crowded (one room, even if on the large size, can get old), and I find myself with the necessity for peace and freedom from interference. The remedy is to take refuge in the outdoors. Because of my own limitations, internal as well as outwardly physical, in hiking I am bound geographically to a specific area—up and down the hill of Sengma, up the next hill to the school, or along the trail to Ghat. In addition to the insanely beautiful mountainous terrain, another redeeming quality of these long, two-three-hour hikes is the delight of finding new paths to explore and categorizing each into my path register. Today I saw an interesting bird due to the shape of its wings—a Himalayan Swift, I believe.

Playing and memorizing Bach every morning for two or three hours is my internal exercise. It wakes me from sleep and begins the day with a familiarity I have known since being a child. An update on my musical endeavors is primarily that Bach V is difficult, not only technically but also due to its mysterious C minor key. It is an intricate work that I must take the time I need to absorb. Hiking and existing in a musically parallel, complicated environment, helps the inspiration. I walked beyond the school today although with a bit of hesitation. When we were threshing, Tika related that he had seen two tigers in the 'area' without the important information about the specific zone. Personally, I don't mind this type of sharing as I am presented with a reason to give wide berth to the physically challenging upper mountain, assuming this is the area of which Tika speaks. The fact that these large, wild cats (Bengal tigers in Nepal) are believed to be solitary in nature, adds to the reasons for my sharing-forgiveness. Along with the monkeys, this is quite a wildlife preserve.

It is October 31st. I am remembering the yearly Halloween party given by a member of our College of Music faculty. Somehow, we always ended up, fully clothed, in the shower for a group photo. Perhaps it is being held tonight.

Another hike to Ghat and again, no *kitabs*. My Namche friends either forgot or left them somewhere unknown to me. I remember to bring back to Sengma gifts from Ghat: potato chips, gum, and sweets for the girls, continuing a streak of bad influence. On the return trail, I pass a smiling gentleman weaving the baskets used by the Sherpa to carry their heavy loads (and for cellists on which to practice). I stop for a moment while he shows me his technique; the baskets are intricate with a delicate pattern, but very strong. Wanting to celebrate the ritual of October, after arriving home I carved a jack-o'-lantern out of a big, green pumpkin found in the cattle stall, put in a candle, and attempted to scare away any evil spirits. Mingma and Pasang loved its jagged smile and the shining light; for me, the Celtic tradition— the beginning of winter and the last month of the summer harvest, anticipated the upcoming move from Khumbu to the Kathmandu valley.

The cattle have been brought down from the mountain and harnessed to help with the hoeing. As I watch the methodical plodding of the beasts as they stride up and down the fields in their makeshift yokes, the method of farming seems from a time gone by. Tika is going to ready the *yup yaks* for a trek with Chongba in a few days, loading them with potatoes for a trek to a lodge in Phakding. I must remember to follow them out of Sengma as I am curious in respect to their path to Ghat. After the stream I so carefully cultivated and Phuti's path which still required climbing, I wonder if there is yet another easier trail for the cattle to climb out of the ravine.

Knowing that Tika will soon be leaving with Chongba, I hope that he returns before it is time for me to go. He is an interesting character, whether sitting with a cup of tea in his hand or out in the field directing the cattle—he is always smiling. Phuti continues her relentless work on the beans and potatoes. She made rice flour today in the old, but most satisfactory way—by rubbing stones together. Everyone's direction is turned toward preparing for the winter months. For Phuti it means storing vegetables for the days when the ground is frozen. For Chongba it means the last climb, the last hike before winter really sets in and there are no trekking foreigners. For me, I am going to do my best to relish the last two weeks in Sengma before moving on to warmer climes—Nagarkot. Bach VI awaits. After good preparation, I am ready to begin in earnest the last of the six. Now it is forward and onward to project completion.

Looming large is the step involving the ability to leave Khumbu without too much difficulty. Not to be hyperbolic, the Lukla airport strikes me as signaling the End Times—no organization being the main characteristic. If I manage to find a seat on the airplane, I will be lucky; that sort of detail consumes my thoughts. My level of anxiousness is high, but it lies just below the surface in the form of feeling incredibly restless. Chongba reported that Dinesh has organized two tickets from Lukla to Kathmandu which, hopefully, will be waiting for me at the airport. As my two-month history in Sengma has delivered trials and tribulations, I determine that too many things can go wrong—I need to over-prepare. As in getting ready for an important concert, I am resolved to become familiar with the stage that is Lukla. I need a dress rehearsal.

I hike the trail to Lukla in, what I consider, record time—three hours. The walk is upstream for an hour and a half to Ghat, then crossing the river and downstream to Lukla. I want to speak to Dawa at the Himalayan Lodge who, according to Chongba and Dinesh, is in charge of my tickets on the 14th. Chongba plans a flight to Kathmandu on the same day; in which case, it is my hope that we will be on the same plane. He is an 'in-charge' kind of guy; the sort of person who creates an aura of confidence in his abilities. On the other hand, he says, "I will do my best but cannot promise."

It is a beautiful day and difficult to believe that, as I approach Lukla, the path is recognizable as the one I trod two months ago. Entering the village (no planes on the runway to avoid), I find Dawa at the lodge—a large, white stuccoed building with red and blue windows. He assures me, "Yes, there is no problem with your tickets on the 14th." I should have been satisfied, but I am reminded of the story in Luigi Barzini's wonderful book, 'The Italians.'

An American takes a pair of shoes to the Italian shoe shop. When asked if the shoes could be finished by Thursday, the repairman said, "Of course, they will be ready on Thursday." The repairman has no intention of finishing the shoes by Thursday; he just wants you to feel good until Thursday.[30] In Italy, this is not only the way of life but an example of the Italian's huge heart. If I am lucky and my prayers are being answered, the Italian way of thinking has not made its way into the life of Khumbu.

---

30 Barzini, Luigi, *The Italians*, Touchstone, 1996.

After visiting the lodge, I stop by the chaotic scene of an outdoor bazaar—no shops, simply a large, open, disorganized space. As in Namche, all possible items are being sold, from cuts of meat to clothing and to wood—all laid out on the ground. I break down and purchase bread and fruit for Phuti and candy for the girls. As in Namche, a coffee and an egg sandwich at the Everest Coffee Café (a definite culinary departure from my usual fare) is perfect; and I am fortified to complete a few errands. The internet shop is still closed, but the door was open at the post office. Unfortunately, not a soul is in sight behind the counter; however, scattered on the countertop was an assortment of letters and other papers. Ruffling through the collection of mail, I find a letter from a student in Boulder, mailed on September 7. The saying, "better late than never," absolutely holds true. A real letter, written on a tangible sheet of paper in an actual envelope, amounts to receiving the most wonderful gift. Feeling humbled and missed (according to the letter), my steps have a new bounce as I walk back through the village. As I am wearing a Boulder Himalayan Explorer's cap, thus easily being identified as a Boulderite, a gentleman from the Himalayan Explorers Club of this Khumbu area stops me to say 'hello.' A wonderful young man, he directs a volunteer teacher program in Nepal. Pure coincidence yet again, as the September avalanche had prevented the children in Sengma and the neighboring villages from crossing the bridge to Chaurikharka (the closest school); he had intended to give lessons to not only the children but any adults who were interested. He was even scheduled to live in the house at the top of the hill in Sengma. When the funeral at the upper house made it impossible (the first night I had arrived), his lessons had been postponed.

Being intrigued with a description he gives of a painting school in the village, an establishment that also teaches English and Buddhism, I walk down a short path to the Tangka Painting School at Lukla's *gompa*. Tall white prayer flags inscribed with mantras encircle the beautifully decorated building. When the wind blows the many prayers are released into the universe. Two young boys proudly show me their artwork—a warm welcome indeed. As they were in such high spirits, I could not resist buying one of their paintings—a *mandala*. Even though I asked and received a positive response, seeing only groups of boys I could not tell if girls attend the school.

Walking back to Ghat and then onward to Sengma, I look at the mountains across the Dudh Kosi and north to Everest and, for the thousandth time, I cannot believe I am here. I promise to myself that I will try not to have any more anxious thoughts; the status of my leaving Lukla is providing enough for the time being. About the flight and with the same attitude as Dawa, Chongba says, "no problem." He **thinks** the plane will work out; and as I have a reserved ticket, what could go wrong? Hiking back to Sengma, I stop for tea at Mama Phuti's and again at Sonna Mama's (no relationship to anyone in Sengma). How lovely to know these villagers well enough that they invite me into their homes. They chatter away; and I still, after two months, try to figure out the intent from hand gestures and a few Sherpa words. It is all right—I can understand enough.

Bach V is almost memorized; and, as I have begun VI, I have decided to save most of the work on this last suite for the new climate in Nagarkot. Every morning I give myself a performance (audience of none) of Suites I-V and know that soon I will be completing the entire cycle. My schedule for these last two weeks will consist of hiking in the morning after the cello performance, and then practicing again after lunch. I am within sight of fulfillment.

The lack of ability to communicate is still leaving me with quite a few mixed signals. Like all children, Mingma and Pasang want attention, and my playing the cello is not the attention for which they are desperate. I am sure that they mean well, however they can be incredibly annoying at times, hiding my walking stick, pestering me during practicing—plainly wanting to irritate. At moments like these, the monastery idea seems as if it might have been a better choice; but I must admit that I enjoy having the girls around when I am unoccupied. When not at school, they are often alone in the fields, both playing and moving in parallel.

In the meantime, Phuti is continuing to dry vegetables on mats outside for the winter: beans, potatoes, and lettuce/chard, all to be stored in the large brass containers. This preparation for the winter seems to have taken over her day as she is rarely inside. In addition, all the grass to be stored for the cattle has been collected. Chongba went to Kathmandu for business reasons and will take another group of trekkers to the mountains. After those commitments, he promises to return.

Late afternoons have been turning cold and cloudy, then the skies clear at night for sun in the morning—the part of the day when I love beside outside to hike the paths. I am slightly worried about the cold for the cello, the blanket at night still being a useless endeavor. I, however, grab at any straw to feel that I am paying attention to the health of the instrument. I am wearing a coat to practice—not the easiest to move around. I can imagine how cold this house will become in the deep winter. The fire must be constant, giving heat for hours on end. For the moment, all I ask is that it does not rain or snow until I leave Lukla because the planes, having no radar or navigation guidance at the airport, will not leave the ground in inclement weather.

It is November 11, and almost time to leave the valley. Chongba AND Tshering arrive from Kathmandu. Any lingering cloud lifted when Tshering, along with her delightful smile, came up the staircase! Chongba has been hiking Imja Tse, better known as Island Peak—an extension of the ridge coming down off the south end of Lhotse Shar. The peak was named Island Peak in 1953 by members of the British Mount Everest expedition because it appears as an island in a sea of ice when viewed from Dingboche,"[31] across the valley from Namche. A couple of Chongba's trekkers got altitude sickness, so he was able to come home early. He will, in any event, leave tomorrow for Phakding to meet up with another trekking group. Happily, for me, Tshering is in Sengma to lend a helping hand with the plane on Sunday. She is a no-nonsense sort of

---

31 Wylie, Charles, "Everest, 1953", *Himalayan Journal*. 2018, https://en.wikipedia.org/wiki/Imja_Tse.

woman; I have the distinct feeling that she will take things into her own hands, and we will be successful in our return to Kathmandu.

A party of sorts is taking place. From Kathmandu, Tshering brought WHISKY AND **CHICKEN**! I should probably take advantage of the diet of the past two months and become a vegetarian—the regimen would no doubt be much healthier. Tonight, however, the chicken is a glorious deterrent to that way of thought. I am organizing my packing, giving items away to Phuti and the girls. It is good to lighten my load, keeping only necessities for Nagarkot. If Tika returns (he has offered to carry the cello to Lukla), we will leave tomorrow (Friday) for Chaurikharka with the intention that Tshering can visit her mother for an evening. She will travel with me on to Kathmandu, the plane leaving on Sunday. This may be the last night in Sengma.

I speak too soon for it is Friday, and Tika has not returned! As we are depending upon him to carry the cello, our departure from Sengma is delayed. There is still whisky, so all is not lost. Tika arrives on Saturday, smiling and eager to help. Even with the delay, Tshering, along with the whisky and the communication in English, brought the confidence I needed. I am assured that all will transpire on schedule. It only takes a few hours of preparation, and we are ready to leave this little community of which I have been a part for almost three months.

A few tears are shed, and I say good-bye to Phuti and the girls. We are off! It is a beautiful day with the sun shining and the mountains in full display. There are a few clouds, but I am hopeful for tomorrow. Tika is carrying everything—the cello AND the backpack (*zola*) and a few items of his own. "No problem, no heavy," he says, smiling. The hike goes smoothly. Although at a quick pace (Tika feeling no pain whatsoever), Tshering and I have the breath to chat about Kathmandu and my remaining time in Nepal. We stop off in Chaurikharka having arrived in record time—only a little over two hours. One of the last meals in Khumbu is with Tshering's parents—*momos*, a special spicy treat. After lunch, we walk on to Lukla, checking into the Himalayan Lodge. Saying good-bye to

Tika as he heads back to Sengma, I am having difficulties finding the right words. Whenever life was difficult, I only had to spend a moment with his joyous nature. Even though Nepali, he always seemed to understand my jerry-rigged Sherpa skills. The stick he carved will remain with me for the next two weeks; and hopefully, longer. There is much *angst* as, with all friends met and left behind, the possibility of seeing them again is an unknown.

Tonight, there is a party of Chongba's Island Peak trekkers—only four left out of ten due to sickness. After leaving his group in Lukla, he has returned to Sengma; he knows that I am in good hands with Tshering. Two trekkers from the States are at the lodge, one from Atlanta and one from Chicago. It is lovely to meet them and to hear their stories. Both have been climbing, and even though not reaching the top, had good experiences. In my little room I say my last prayer in Khumbu: "Please, no rain tomorrow!"

Befitting my personality, I am up early in the morning, waiting by the runway at the specific location that organizes departing passengers. Tshering arrives, looking well-rested with two coffees and the two tickets. It is hard to imagine that I am leaving and now have in my hand a take-away coffee, another first. The logic is not lost on me, however, for I realize that no matter how much I wanted coffee during the past months, a singular coffee would not have been worth a three-hour hike. I spend some time taking a photo of the gentleman and his son taking the larger rocks off the runway—an incoming plane is arriving. After the plane stops, they rush out again to remove more rocks before the next plane takes off. They are both on their own as I see no signal, no green light—nothing to indicate that the runway is safe for them to do their work. A plane is about to leave, but Tshering tells me that it is not ours (I wonder how she knows, for the ticket does not show a flight number or airline, only a time of departure which is long past). There is a lack of understanding about the cello ticket; but then, if it parallels the trip to Lukla, it will be in the aisle. Dawa arrives to say 'good-bye' and tells me, "It looks good." All engines go.

A Ghorka plane arrives—this is it! Tshering and I take our

seats in a very small plane, probably no more than 12 passengers. Dawa crams my cello into the aisle as before, along with the many backpacks of my fellow passengers. Taking off by plane is no less exciting than my arrival over two months ago.

A better description I could not have written. "With the propellers on fine pitch and the brakes locked, the pilot pushes the throttles to maximum, only releasing the brakes as the locked wheels begin to slide. The plane seems to 'hop' over the bend in the runway, then flies to the end, using the updraft to take off. With a glorious rush the plane bounces into the air."[32] More cotton wool is given us for the ears (any conversation is impossible), and we fly past the monumental mountains and valleys of Khumbu. The short flight was anything but smooth, but we land in Kathmandu about 30 minutes later to many onboard cheers. Leaving the little plane, Tshering and I are met with air that is gloriously warm. I can put away the long underwear. Thank you, Buddha, for a safe trip back to the city. I am a step closer.

---

32 McGuinness, *Trekking in the Everest Region*, 147.

PART FOUR

RETURNING HOME
Khangba Lokyi खंग्बा लोक्यी

Remembering the feeling of being alone on my arrival in Kathmandu more than two months ago, how wonderful it is to see Dinesh at the airport with a waiting taxi. He wants to give a helping hand on the next leg of this adventure. It is a short taxi ride to Nagarkot; and the taxi is large, a quasi-SUV, able to accommodate four passengers and the cello with ease. Nagarkot is a relatively small village on the edge of Kathmandu's valley—a village on the top of a hill surrounded by terraced land on all sides and known for scenic views of the Himalayas. The taxi driver, speaking rather good English, is telling me all of this, even relaying the fact that the village is only sixteen miles from the airport—"You can even walk" he tells me, giving the distinct impression that he had other things to do besides driving up the mountain to Nagarkot.

The village, at a little over 7,100 feet, is reached by a paved, but dusty road all the way up the hill. There is an occasional bus, car, or motorcycle kicking up dust as it passes, or causing us to stop when the road is exceptionally narrow. I pass the time by relaying to Dinesh the adventures of the past two months. As we climb higher, we find ourselves in the middle of pine forests or terraced land. It is a peaceful setting with a few buildings and a constantly winding road. As we reach the village, a row of tourist buses reminds me that this is the go-to area for any day-tripper from Kathmandu.

We arrive at my destination for the next two weeks, the Galaxy Hotel of Nagarkot. Imagine my surprise when I step out of the taxi and can see the mountains of the Khumbu region to the east. Dinesh tells me that in the mornings, when it is usually clear, I'll be able to see Mt. Everest in the northeast, the Annapurna range on the west, and the beauty of the Lantang-Jugal range to the north of the Kathmandu valley. In fact, Nagarkot, a popular tourist spot as I gather by the number of buses, is known for its hiking trails; and, as I have a few maps, I will definitely try a few.

For me, after two months in the Khumbu area, the hotel is the most luxurious place I have ever seen—the buildings in a reddish pink, and in layers due to the terracing of the hills. The lodge is furnished with a restaurant and a BAR! I have serious concerns that a material life is important to my comfort. Did I not spend over two months with a family that had little, but that 'little' was all they needed to be happy and comfortable? Dinesh and Tshering help with my arrival at the welcome desk (the language is Nepali, but a few words are spoken in English); and over a cup of tea in the restaurant, a simple, small space with colorful cloths covering the tables, we discuss the next steps. They will reappear on December 1. We will then return to Kathmandu in ample time for my plane on the 3rd. After many hugs and an invitation for a farewell dinner at their home when I return, they say their 'good-byes'. The taxi takes them away, the car dwindling in the distance as it leaves Nagarkot and begins the climb downward. I am alone again, however this time, with the place and the people, I am surrounded with a different energy. The energy notwithstanding, as I was in Sengma, I am enveloped with a landscape—the beauty of which I will never become disenchanted.

The smiling young men that greet me at the bar (yes, I went straight there) inform me that for just a short walk of 15 minutes I can be at the Club Himalaya. A relatively deluxe hotel, in their business center I can use the phone and WI-FI. With this sense of possible communication with my family, I am overcome with a sense of happiness that has been long overdue. The final gift is that I can remain for two weeks in the same space—no moving about necessary. My home is on the lower level of the main building and down quite a few steps. Being a separate room on the side of the hotel, it includes a little garden of potted rhododendrons and a real bathroom (my latest desire is one of never wanting to see another outhouse or squat toilet). Adjacent to a patio with rock walls covered with orange pyrostegia and pink/red bougainvillea (evidently winter plants in Nepal), the room is quite delightful with two rather comfortable beds, windows on all sides, and ELECTRIC lights. Facing east, the cottage is also perfect for the morning view of the mountains.

At a time like this, life can be defined by more than just 'good.' 'Undeservedly,' 'unmerited,' and 'excessive,' are the words that come to mind. I smell the aroma of the winter flowers; and above all, I feel the warmth of the wind coming off the hilltop. There will no longer be an urge to cover my cello with blankets. That action had, however, slightly eased a desperate mind while weathering the cold.

The Galaxy sits on the top of a tall, terraced hill, sloping into a valley. I am truly relaxing for the first time in two and a half months—the air clear, the sky blue, and the hotel welcoming. The Kathmandu airport is nearby (even walkable according to the cab driver); its proximity signaling a certain simplicity to whatever lies ahead. It being mid-afternoon, a short walk into the village will satisfy my curiosity to see what is there—as it turns out, not a tremendous amount. I walk past a few pink, multi-storied buildings and guest houses, a bank, and a little shop with film—but those few buildings are enough. Looking down into the valley the intricate terraced land is phenomenally precise in keeping to the curvature of the hills. Every inch of land is being cultivated. At this time of year, some terraces (I am assuming rice) are bare, and others are overflowing with the yellow of the mustard plant. I am reading in my little brochure handed to me at the desk that this is the land of the Newars, people who make up over half the population of this area around Kathmandu. All are Nepali speaking, but also have their own Newar language. I have literally left the Sherpa way of life behind me.

Investigating the hotel restaurant for dinner, and for its atmosphere and advertised home cooking, I find the ambiance enhanced by three young musicians playing Nepali music on typical Nepalese instruments: a *lumu*; a *madal*, hand drum; and what appears to be *Jhyamta*, hand cymbals. They are sitting in front of the menu board—the words in English and written in chalk and script.

>DAY SPECIAL
>
>Hash Brown potato. Oven fresh
>
>Bread. Eggs any style. Tea
>
>or Coffee. Cup Rs 85/
>
>A PLACE WHERE YOU DREAM TO
>
>BE
>
>GALAXY HOTEL + RESTAURANT

This seems like a breakfast menu, but I see EGGS. I am ok with this. The home cooking passes the test, it being without frills but still delicious. Unfortunately, and I cannot believe I am saying this, I might be missing the lack of chilis in the preparation. Enjoying my dinner while being serenaded, it could be said that I am in paradise, and perhaps even dreaming.

After a wonderful night's sleep, it is sunrise, and I am standing on the edge of my little garden—the beginning of my first entire day away from Khumbu. For the first time in a few months, I am filled with the energy that comes from being around others. A half hour earlier, I woke up because of an unaccustomed knock on my door, evidently an amenity given to all the guests in the hotel to remind everyone that at daybreak the views are at their best. The sun is coming up, and the Himalayas are emerging from the gray. A line of the white-covered mountains is coming into view— even Mt. Everest, being far to the east, is still somehow visible.

White, puffy clouds, with the mountains peering over their tops, are trying to seize my attention, and are failing. For the unfolding scene, my room is in the perfect position. Contemplating that I had been, for a time, living in that panorama, this view is the ultimate consolation prize.

After more eggs, I decide to explore the terraces below. Walking down the mountainside with its contours (a Master of Design with some of the terraces intricately curved), I am suddenly besieged by children begging for food—groups of youngsters popping up from time to time as I go down the hill. It is a strange juxtaposition as one would expect beggars of any age in more of a city environment. I suppose with the coming of tourists, comes the knowledge that these outsiders have more to share. Coming into a small village, I decide to turn back. I pass by a group of men brushing the road clear in preparation for laying down tar, a large paving machine standing idly by (I am speaking of the men using small brushes, the type of which you would see in a kitchen—a whisk).

Returning to my room, the fancy hotel Club Himalaya is next on the agenda. In the past two months, I conquered death-defying trails in order to go from point A to B; now it is a short fifteen-minute walk to the phone and email (the family calls must wait due to the time difference). After a little message-writing, I stop by the bank for some more rupees. After investigating a little roadside stand with books and souvenirs, I returned to the Club for a late lunch in a distinctly classy restaurant (pizza, always a good choice). This is all a trifle too civilized.

My cello is not forgotten nor the goal of getting to the last page of my Bach score. My schedule is slightly changed: breakfast, a hike, a gentle stroll into the village, lunch, Bach—an extremely relaxed schedule. Every day there is work on the sixth and final suite, this work in the joyous and exuberant key of D Major, again complementing my mood in Nagarkot. It is in quick time, a rush to the end.

PRÉLUDE

I have an intricate, yet fabulous schedule for the sixth, although some might call the timetable a wee bit overdone in its complexity. Essentially, as outlined at the very beginning of this project, each movement is divided into sections—each section practiced in turn. In the case of this suite, there are many divisions, consequently requiring an elaborate daily routine.

In creating this project, one question has always been the altitude—would living in higher elevations affect the performance of the suites, musically or technically. The altitude, I am convinced, has given me a sense of lightness; and that feeling has transferred to the suites. The *tempi* are brisker and sprightlier in general. For me, a huge change, especially in this sixth suite, has been to take out the heaviness of the phrase and its harmony that one often hears in performance. I want to imply the harmonies—to 'touch and lift' rather than to announce, "this is the harmony; I am giving it weight so you can understand." For example, breathing life into the beautiful and moving melody of the Sarabande of this sixth suite is my goal. Implying the harmony is the answer.

SARABANDE

As I am beginning to play through all the suites, it is taking less effort to become immersed in the uniqueness, the internal beauty of each one. In Sengma, this individuality was supported because of the pervading undercurrents of life, and how I was being affected. As a result, the character of each suite has been built on a strong foundation; and, overall, the foundation on which to live the rest of my life.

The hikes every morning are fantastically interesting. There has been not a drop of rain. In Nagarkot, I am told, the monsoon weather ended its grip quite a while ago. Several villages are within easy hiking distance; and with no cliffs and no waterfalls to confuse, I have time to devote to the skill of hiking in the uncomplicated vertical. I may even be winning the challenge. The dirt trails are simple, meandering downward alongside the terraced land until reaching the few simple structures of a neighboring village. This area, aside from the village of Nagarkot itself, seems very poor and extremely underdeveloped. Bhataphur and Tittake are two such villages at the bottom of the valley, an area in which there is a feeling of having been forgotten. The houses are like those in Khumbu—stone (although some have been stuccoed), with the backs of some outlying structures against the steep, terraced hillside. Most have thatched or tin roofs. For winter, I am surprised at the number of flowers as I descend: bougainvillea, fields of yellow mustard, red poinsettia, rhododendrons of all colors, the beautiful orange pyrostegia (also on my patio) which is often pouring over the balconies of the houses in town.

Images on the dirt trails can be captured in pictures: a woman hysterically crying standing alongside a man and child with no indication that they notice; a gigantic black cow with very short, curved horns sitting under a shelter, fixed to a wooden post with a wire through its nostrils (could have been a Gaur, the Indian bison, the largest known wild cattle on the planet);[33] and the working villagers along the many, terraced paths. I am always alone as I walk down; but the begging children are sometimes in hiding, sensing when I arrive at their 'station' on the trail. Having gained familiarity with my daily schedule, the group of five or six children

---

33 "Gaur – the tiger killer," https://thewebsiteofeverything.com/animals/mammals/Artiodactyla/Bovidae/Bos/Bos-frontalis.html.

are now armed with sticks (pretending to be tollgate operators I am guessing) and refusing to let me pass. Once I was so uncomfortable that I turned around, being followed by shrieks and noise. If I could speak Hindi or Newar, I doubt the situation would have improved. For the last few days, I have found new paths to explore; although in some way, I am sad to not understand these encounters.

Walks in this unique new setting, sunset on my patio with a glass of wine reading a book found at the photo shop, the morning knock on the door—all translates into a wonderful transition to returning home. It is almost too idyllic. The change to Nagarkot gives every appearance of being a new realignment. Clearly a welcome transformation in terms of verbal communication, this redirection is also returning something that has been missing for the past few months—communication through music. Being defined by the music I perform has been a great part of my identity since youth. Not having that association has been distressing, to say the least. I must admit that from the beginning of this project, I did not anticipate, nor did I especially desire, a tremendous amount of communication (social or musical) during this adventure, thinking back to the monastery cell in Tibet. When confronted with no interchange whatsoever except the dialog I could conjure up with myself (in music and otherwise), a certain disillusionment took over—perhaps the romantic notion of purposeful isolation is too difficult for one without the personal history or training. Complete social isolation can be quite numbing. In Sengma, the lack of discourse through speaking, writing, and music was complete—the latter, until today.

I met a group of six American students at the restaurant—volunteers at St. Theresa's in Calcutta. Having heard me practicing, they asked if they could listen. After lunch they sat outside on the terrace next door while I performed all six suites in my garden—the first time in almost three months making music for others. The achievement, every suite in order, lasted just over two and a half hours. The dialogue with these listeners produced responses of fascination and enthusiasm. No one moved except for the occasional sip of wine; and there was no smile greater than mine. Here we are, looking out over the terraced hills, the Himalayas in the distance—an entire range before us, with Bach singing from the hillside. I finally had an audience.

The Bach initiative, the thread that has wound through my journey, is completed. My meditation project was an interesting one and served its purpose, at least in short spurts, or perhaps my performances of the suites are meditations in themselves for I am remembering the landscape from whence the waterfall was born. Several days are left in Nepal, and I have almost crossed off all the XX's on my calendar, the circled date gradually coming within reach. I do not think I have ever felt the need to mark the days in this manner, and hopefully never will again. Ending this adventure in Nagarkot has been a needed shift, transporting me from an exhausting and formidable experience to a brighter day.

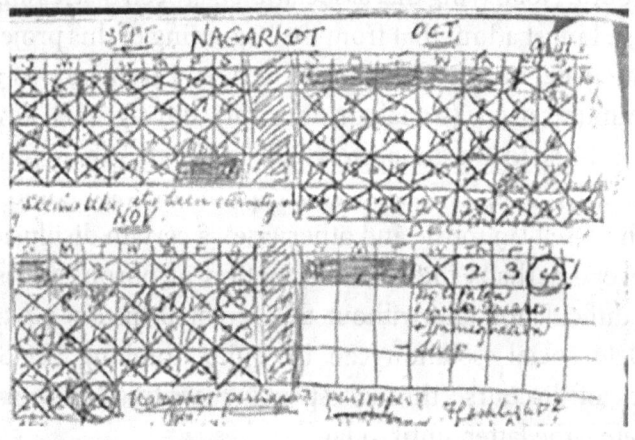

In this little village I have met a wonderful assortment of people: the gentleman who refuses to turn on the computer at the Club Himalaya because "the sky is cloudy," the wonderful musicians who play during every meal, the gentleman who knocks on my door every morning even when fog obstructs the view, the boy at the photo shop who keeps trying to sell me a 'fancy camera' for a dollar, and those staying at the hotel—the American students, a young girl from Brisbane on her way to London, Vibé from

Denmark, Jim from Ireland, Jezz from Vancouver, John and Judy from Australia—an eclectic slice of the globe. There is no longer the isolation that shadowed me during the months in Khumbu. With this realignment, it is time to go home.

December 1st has arrived. A boy from the front desk arrives at my door to tell me the news. In one hour, Dinesh will appear with a taxi to take me back to Kathmandu. I will miss Nagarkot for the serenity it allowed; the village was, however, one step closer to returning home. In these three months, I have mentally composed a living composition in a subtle sonata form: an exposition of apprehension, a development of distress, a short peaceful transition returning to an overwrought recapitulation, and ending with a tranquil coda. Perhaps this creation would be more recognizable if I wrote it all down.

Dinesh arrives, and soon we are back on the road—the dusty, dirt track going through the forest of pine, returning to where it all began. I look forward to the vibrant activity of Kathmandu with its colors and clashing sounds. I will have two full days before the plane departs to see and hear what I missed three months ago.

Dinesh has made reservations at the same hotel—the Nirvana Garden; the lodging still unbelievably surrounded by blooming flowers. I see a smiling Curry and Bizet at the welcome desk in exactly the same spot, inspiring me to question if they have moved from their position in the past three months. It is a homecoming with welcoming smiles all around. When I arrived back in early September and entered my room, the roaches and flies were unwelcome guests, intruding on my space. Now I return months later and seeing a few roaches scurry around, I would probably even feed the little insects if I had some of Phuti's potatoes in my pocket. It has taken a great deal to change my attitude; hopefully, the change will be long-lasting.

Chongba is also in Kathmandu, but it is doubtful that I will see him before I leave. Always the businessman, he is looking into new treks to lead into the mountains. The Sherpas' life is perpetually non-stop. When we spoke in Sengma, Chongba mentioned that he would like to obtain a visa for Phuti to visit the States, and especially to see Pemba in Boulder. Phuti wants to see America, Chongba says. "She has never seen an escalator."

For the rest of today and tomorrow, I am on my own. On the final full day in Kathmandu, December 3rd, Dinesh would like to be my guide in Patan, one of Nepal's three largest cities and across the Bagmati. He is not only an amazing young man, but his knowledge of the city leaves no stone unturned. I am thankful to become a tourist once again, seeing more of Kathmandu before my exodus. After the visit to Patan, Dinesh and Tshering have invited me to their home for dinner. They have asked if I could bring the cello!

It is mid-afternoon after my arrival from Nagarkot, and I am walking the streets of Thamel with a brisker, happier step this time. I am feeling light, being aware of a very different sensation—inside and out. Even though I am wandering the same streets as in early September, everything seems illuminated. The energy of Kathmandu is electric and exhilarating. Without the constant worry of before, the blur of the crowds in the street, the shops, the restaurants—the haze is gone. Looking everywhere, I see a different Thamel, and yet the district is still inundated with the adventurous souls preparing to trek, and the many vendors helping to smooth the way. Thamel will remain the hub of Nepal's thriving backpackers' industry. It is a district filled with color, anxious energy and frantic activity, the people rushing around in the street preparing for their own approaching adventure. In September, I was such a novice. Even though still a newcomer to this compulsion to climb, I now walk down these streets as a member of the community. I believe I understand just a fraction of the motivation.

I walk along the still-crowded main pedestrian street; and seeing a sign for pizza, walked in. The Roadhouse Café is swarming with young people; their backpacks slung over the backs of chairs. The café is an inviting place with Nepali wall decorations, many wooden tables, and an outside patio overflowing with greenery. The smell of pizza cooking in a wood-burning oven is enough reason to end my search for an early dinner. Joining two young women from New York, we chat about their up-coming trip to the Annapurna region. Speaking about the 'anxious energy' of the typical backpacker, in these two women I am finding a distinct similarity with myself when first arriving in Thamel—mentally trying to deal with the unknown future. For me, it was only an eternity ago.

The next day is devoted to business. I must handle the necessary bureaucracy for the trip home. In the morning, after tea and *gwaramari,* a fried, bread-like dumpling (typical breakfast food), the Department of Immigration awaits. A new face stands behind the welcome desk of the Nirvana, a gentleman by the name of Adesh. In five minutes, a taxi is waiting outside. My driver is very quiet and calm as we drive through chaotic, frantic streets. The elephants of my previous visit are now joined by another—all three ridden by young boys, colorful blankets in the place of saddles. The elephants are standing still but, on the diagonal, blocking all traffic. Each vehicle, save for the very adroit motorcyclist and rickshaw driver, is at a standstill. After much honking, the elephants and their riders lumber off, and we continue on our way. All paved roads seem to lead to the Immigration building, a multi-storied pinkish structure. The organization inside is quite good—only short lines awaited me. My application, a document for travel, is approved within minutes with no questions asked. The government really wants to make sure I am leaving the country.

Waiting outside is my very patient taxi driver. Next on the agenda is a quick ride, only five minutes away, to the Thai Air office to confirm my documents and to receive the actual international tickets to Colorado. All is in order. The cello has a bona fide and actual seat instead of one in the aisle. Both ventures having gone so smoothly, I decide to walk back to the hotel for lunch and an afternoon of seeing the sights. In short order I am surrounded by the distinctive shops of Thamel. I stroll along, enjoying the colorful flags and signs, and from the restaurants the smells of every cuisine imaginable. I stopped only once at the Pilgrim's Bookstore for a sci-fi adventure, a must-have for the trip home.

I return to my hotel room after a very late lunch and decide to play through Suite VI, just to keep it in my fingers. As luck would have it, no one knocked on the ceiling or walls to quiet me down. After another, longer walk, trying to expand my familiar boundaries, I return to the menu of the Roadhouse Café for dinner, my purpose being to make a transition to the culinary choices of Colorado—no more *dal bhat* for the time being. It is quieter tonight—only four or five other people in the restaurant. As a result, I sit by myself with a Roadhouse Burger and fries, and another glass of wine. All decisions having been made, a peaceful evening lies ahead as I begin to feel whole once more.

In the morning, after tea and toast, Dinesh arrives with his car for our last outing in the city. We are off to Patan's Durbar Square. I plan to enjoy my final full day in Nepal. Everything I need to make the trip home—my backpack and the cello, all is ready to go. Even Tika's stick will not be forgotten.

After first arriving in Kathmandu, I visited several of the main religious temples and squares in Kathmandu. It is only fitting that before I leave, after having spent three months in the sacred landscape of Khumbu, a region of Sherpa Buddhist tradition and religious practice, that I spend some time at one last religious site—Patan's Durbar Square in the center of the city of Lalitpur, across the river Bagmati. Lalitpur is one of Nepal's largest cities and said to be one of the oldest Buddhist cities in the world.

We arrive in Patan and walk to the outside of the square. Immediately, we find ourselves in the middle and clamor of a large shopping district, with disorganized and rather chaotic shops existing together along the sides of the square itself, selling to the tourist and local trade all forms of statues, bells, wheels, food, and household goods. As soon as we enter the red-tiled pavement of the square proper, the quiet is all-encompassing. Few tourists are noticeable. There are at least 55 temples in this area, some four and five-tier structures, some more egg-shaped—Hindu and Buddhist together. I am surprised at the pagoda-like architecture of some of the Buddhist temples; in my mind, this style was reserved solely for sacred Hindu shrines. Wandering through the square, the physical number of temples and statues is staggering. Rows and rows of temples are crowded together, some guarded by sculptures of lions or elephants and surfaced with golden adornments. Nevertheless, all are embellished in every conceivable fashion. [34]

We stroll throughout the maze of structures; and, after a quick lunch of tea and *momos* at a neighboring café, a ten-minute walk takes us to the Golden Temple and Buddhist monastery from the early 15th century. Again, in the style of a pagoda, another name for this shrine is the Rat Temple. Luckily, the rodents (there are evidently many inside) do not venture outside. I decline to enter as even small mice are to me terrorizing. In addition, leather not being allowed inside the courtyard, one must be barefoot (bare feet and rats are not a winnable combination). Dinesh tells me that there are a huge number of artifacts inside—that I am missing a tremendous amount by not entering the enclosure. I have nothing else to add; his rational declaration that we would not encounter a rat was not sound logic. The temple, however, is a beautiful structure from the outside. With gold plates at the front and with glittering brass decorations, it is literally shining. Interestingly, not only in Patan but also in Kathmandu, the most fascinating woodcarvings on Nepali temples, as can also be seen on this Buddhist Golden Temple, are on the roof struts—erotic scenes fill the spaces. The themes have a Tantric element, a clear connection to the intermingling of Tibetan Buddhism and Hindu beliefs in Nepal. The real purpose is, however, unclear. [35]

I convince Dinesh to come with me to visit the nearby Tibetan Refugee Carpet Market in Patan, thinking I might send a carpet home to Boulder. As its name suggests, the Tibetan Refuge Camp was begun in 1960 to give the Tibetan refugees a productive life in creating and selling carpets. This world-famous Nepali industry is almost completely run by the refugee families here

---

34   "Patan Durbar Square," https://en.wikipedia.org/wiki/Patan_Durbar_Square.
35   World Travel Family, "Golden Temple Nepal. Rat Temple in Kathmandu," https://worldtravelfamily.com/rat-temple-nepal/.

in the Kathmandu valley.[36] In quite a dilapidated, brick-walled building, we see most of the processes of rug-making: piles of raw wool in one room, groups of women spinning the yarn in another with weavers at the looms—all in the larger space of the factory. Children are happily climbing over the wooden machines—a sign of shared family operations. The men in the building seem to be solely in charge of the sales division. Knowing that I can live without a Nepali carpet is telling me that my travels as a guest in this country are ending. I just want to go home—almost desperately. I have only been absent for three months; the question, "why such desperation?" must wait for an answer.

When I first arrived in Kathmandu, I labeled Tshering and Dinesh as my 'new best friends.' They were there for me at the beginning and are here for me at the end. These two lovely people have invited me for dinner at their apartment tonight—the evening before leaving Nepal. The Last Supper. Being able to spend this time together in their home is the most wonderful, private conclusion to this journey. We share a bottle of wine and a delicious dinner: rice with a wonderfully spicy vegetable curry, even spicier chutneys, and a flatbread known as *papadamu*; after which I play for them a few dances from the first suite, the joyful G Major. Dinesh presents me with email messages that he has brought home from his company—mail that had arrived in September. To comment about the delay is not important. A simple "thanks" must do. We take some photos for a fitting finale.

All the paperwork to leave Nepal is in hand, and on December 4th, Tshering, Dinesh and I leave for the airport with the cello and a much lighter backpack—the unneeded is being left behind. After arrival, Tshering and I head into the building, move through security and the x-ray machine receiving a stamp for the cello (the machine had the same Sharpie-printed, crooked sign), and proceed to the desk to check-in for the flight (all was in order) and, finally, to the departure gate. As there is time to kill until boarding, we

---

36 "Patan: Tibetan Refuge Camp," https://www.raonline.ch/pages/np/visin/np_patan01g.html.

decide to go outside to visit with Dinesh one last time. We leave the waiting area by way of a nearby exit door and catch up with him. A few tears and an emotional 'good-bye' end our final encounter. Tshering and I go back to the gate by way of the same exit door. It is curious that we did not have to repeat the security procedures, even after having been outside. I must say that the Kathmandu airport has a rather lax security system. I will continue to turn those prayer wheels, if only in my mind.

During the next two days, I am arriving at the airports of three months ago—this time in reverse. Tired yet jubilant, I arrive in Denver and am overjoyed to see some of my students waiting for me at the gate with balloons. I am home! The three months in Nepal have come to an end. There will be time to ponder what it has meant; for the moment, I can relish the fact that my Bach project is complete, that my obsession with Everest has been satisfied, and I have met some wonderful human beings in an intense environment. For now, it is time to thank Tshering and Dinesh, Pemba, Phuti and Chongba for all they have done for me. Only one truly sad thing happened at the very end. I was so anxious to leave the plane, I left Tika's walking stick in the overhead compartment. I miss that stick even now for it had protected and saved me from many a mishap. It was one of the true items of stability that got me through. I will use a hyperbolic way of description in saying that it probably saved my life. Thank you, Tika.

CONCLUSION
Thedoma थादोम्

Above all: That Bach *is* life and *was* my life for three months in Nepal. That Bach is no more, no less, a heart that beats. That Bach, when seen in solitude, shows itself. That Bach is as powerful as the highest peak in the world.

What I have learned about the things I can do: Build a fire. Wash clothes on rocks. Eat *dal bhat* twice a day. Work out solutions to large problems. Find extreme satisfaction with Bach in the mountains. Wash once a week in a large bowl and realize this is adequate. Learn a great deal about practicing and memorizing. Live without material goods and conveniences. Trek for hours because of what is at the end. Hike like a Sherpa (hand on hip, walk on the side of steps if possible). Enjoy having someone carry the cello. Know that I am still a master at scheduling. Live without a phone and a computer.

What I have learned about the things I cannot do: Thresh wheat with a primitive threshing tool (I like to think I could learn). Eat boiled potatoes every day. Live without friends and family. Hold back fear and desolation. Live without the occasional chocolate. Have patience with pestering kiddos. Live without books. Delight in the outhouse experience. Hike as fast as Phuti. Love landing and taking off from Lukla (the landing strip was paved in 2001). Walk among rats. Nothing else.

When I arrived back in Boulder, I was curious to see if the isolation and contemplation of the past three months would continue to inform my life in my home and university—to return to the complex nature of communication that makes up life in America. It was impossible to believe after such an experience, that I could settle back into routines, keeping the wheels turning; but here I am. As I have said, I did not choose this project to perform the suites on the concert stage; the goal was to discover what the Bach suites could teach me, and then be prepared to share whatever knowledge I learned. Nevertheless, I did play the suites in informal settings; and, of course, every day for my students.

Without realizing in 1999, this concept of complete and utter focus (in Nepal it was the practice of meditation) became a mainstay of my teaching. The definition of 'practice' in the *Cambridge Dictionary* is, "the act of doing something regularly or repeatedly to improve your skill at doing it." Musicians live with the idea that we must spend hours a day in 'practice,' determined to repeat the technique or musical phrase over and over until we have a semblance of perfection. Instead of always 'repeating' when in the practice room, a much better idea is to train yourself to focus. If you can free your mind of the everyday thoughts, the goal is achievable very quickly; little repetition is needed.

I wrote an article in *Strings* on this very topic in 2012. In my music student days, I knew that focus was important; that it was not necessary to practice many hours a day if one could just fixate intensely on the task at hand. For this article, I decided to try an experiment with my students at the University of Colorado Boulder. It was to be a three-week project, beginning with a student's repertoire at a certain point but lacking consistency in performance. The student timed his repertoire, the total being the number of minutes it took for him to play everything through **once**. The amount of time for this student's repertoire was 32 minutes. The student was to practice for three weeks; however, instead of his usual five hours a day he was required to practice daily for only 32 minutes. No mistakes and no repeating—once through everything.

The experiment was frustrating, but at the end of the third week, he discovered with great satisfaction that his sense of focus had heightened, and that he was accomplishing more in the practice room than ever before. In a sense, he was meditating—separating his mind from the inane and focusing only on being in the present. This is a technique that could be helpful in accomplishing many tasks of life, not just in the music practice room.[37]

A friend recently asked, "Twenty years after this experience, why are you writing about it now; and, understanding how you felt during those three months, what are your feelings today?" Believe it or not, I am still sorting it all out. I know that I needed time to put those very difficult three months into perspective—to reflect on that particular journey. The difficulties of those three months stayed with me for years; they are still with me in many ways. It was impossible to create an opening into that other world—that sphere was always lying just beyond. I had to remember that I had chosen the solitude; I did not, however, choose the loneliness that came from having been surrounded by others and yet living in complete isolation.

As Messner, did I see deep inside myself? I do believe that the complexity of those months made for a stronger, more resilient human being and gave me a certain permission to become even more adventurous—to take more chances. In this regard, my desire to erase the downside, the bad, and to remember the benefit, the good, has been an ongoing and necessary effort. Because of this effort, I have come to realize that it is time to lay it all to rest—to put the experience down on paper. Sophocles, in 'Oedipus Rex', said it best: "I have no desire to suffer twice, in reality, and then in retrospect."[38]

My feelings today? I realize that nothing good can come of remorse; and that I cannot allow myself many regrets. If there is

---

[37] Glyde, Judith, "Practice Perfectly, not Practice Makes Perfect," *Strings*, July 2012, No.207, 34.

[38] Sophocles, *Oedipus Rex*, Dudley Fitts and Robert Fitzgerald (transll), Harcourt, Inc., 1949, 1977.

one, in choosing to place myself into social isolation and being overcome, at times, by my own despondency, I was rendered emotionally numb; and this was not constructive. I could argue that Bach benefitted from the circumstance; in which case, that is sufficient. Above all, I have pride--pride in that I was able to meet the challenge that was Bach—that was Khumbu. The beauty of Khumbu and its people will remain with me always.

I have not seen Tshering, Dinesh, Chongba, Mingma or Pasang these past twenty-four years although one day I hope that reunion will occur. I was in touch with Tshering and Dinesh for a while in the effort to bring them to the States (and with the news of a new baby); I hope that they were eventually successful in that effort and that their family is happy and well. Chongba succeeded in a visa for Phuti for I saw her a few years later in the kitchen of Pemba's establishment in Boulder, the *Sherpa's Adventure Restaurant* (I am sure it was still "Phuti's food"). Pemba, the instigator of this entire journey, continues to be a successful businessman, developing new enterprises: another restaurant in Boulder, the *Fuji Café & Bar*, *Sherpa Chai* (the recipe coming from Pemba's mother and known to be the best chai on the market), and other ventures. Significantly, he has used his success to help the Sherpas in the Khumbu region. After I left his village, Pemba built a new bridge from Chaurikharka to Sengma, replacing the original one that had been destroyed in the avalanche, cutting the distance from the three-hour hike we walked to thirty minutes. With donations from Pemba and others, a small hydro-electric facility was built in Sengma with the ability to power a number of light bulbs; and, after the 2015 disastrous earthquake in Nepal, the tremors causing destruction in the Khumbu region, Pemba was instrumental in bringing supplies to the victims and in rebuilding his land.[39]

---

39 Sherpa, Pemba, with James McVey, *Bridging Worlds, A Sherpa's Story* Sherpa Publications, 2019.

I truly believe that life is an adventure. Like a piece of driftwood, it waits for the next wave. In 2023, twenty-four years after an implausible adventure in Khumbu, I feel the same compulsion to be self-determining—to have the freedom to undertake interesting and valuable projects. I am forging on with life in the same fashion I tackled three months in Nepal, taking the challenges as they come, seeking peace to reflect on what is happening around me and flourishing from what I learn. My experience in Sengma will remain the adventure of a lifetime—the most remarkable journey I have ever weathered. The beauty of Khumbu and its people, especially my Sherpa family, will remain with me always. Speaking of beauty and adventures, I should write another story about restoring a house in southern Italy.

APPENDIX

RECIPES FROM PHUTI'S KITCHEN

The Sherpa home is centered around food and community. If people come by at mealtimes, the food will always be shared. The fire, the hearth in the center of the dwelling, is the Sherpa home. All food is cooked over the open wood fire and is generally spicy with the regular addition of chilis and garlic. These fresh spices are hung in baskets above the hearth. The ease of creating a fire with the air from the bellows was beyond my grasp. Phuti was a master. The roaches were always difficult to cope with, but it is unbelievable how I became accustomed to almost anything. A lesson in frugality is always worthwhile. Two of the kitchen tools were made with the simplest of materials: a grater was made by punching holes with a nail on a piece of metal and affixing it to a piece of wood; and a broom, by tying branches together.

In the fall, work is centered around a garden of primarily potatoes, beans, and wheat. In November, in mid-afternoon, everyone takes a break from the fields, sits, and eats boiled potatoes. The potatoes are cooked, skinned (the peels are saved for the cattle) and eaten whole. I looked forward to this ritual every day for it was a time when I became a part of the community. These recipes are my favorites, the straightforward wording and comments taken unchanged from my journal, the cooking instructions written while watching Phuti in her kitchen.

- Potato Curry – *Rudok*. Mash potatoes until smooth consistency. Put into about two cups of boiling water. Separate. Boil and stir. Take out some water and add spices (onions, chiles, etc.). Stir potato mixture furiously. The water will be absorbed. Add a bit of flour as you stir. The mixture will become a bit elastic. Take off heat. Serve with sauce. Comment: this curry has a rather strange texture.
- Fry in oil some green leafy vegetables. Add cooked rice. Good, easy variation.
- *Luma Pourrie*– Rice flour, baking powder, salt, 2 eggs, water, sugar. Drop into oil by making a circular motion and deep fry. Sprinkle with confectioners' sugar.
- *Momo*. Chop up cabbage or greens. In wok, cook crushed garlic and chilis in oil. Add cabbage, curry powder to wok. Cook until cooked down for 10-15 minutes. Make dough of flour and water. Roll thinly, then cut into circles about 2 ½-3" in diameter. Fill with cabbage mixture, close and crimp tightly shut. Place momos, face down, in top of an oiled double boiler. Cook about 10 minutes then fry in a little oil. Serve with spicy tomato sauce.
- Green chilis. Slice the top and put in a jar of water (like pickling). Eat plain or combine for cooking.
- Pancakes. Make watery pancake mixture. Cook in a little oil like regular pancakes. Serve with sauteed spicy green vegetables.
- *Mai-Ta Toppa*. Mix flour and water. Roll out to a very thin square and divide dough for easy handling. Fold the square 3 times and cut into ¼ "wide lengths. This will look like fat pasta. Keeping pasta floured, heat oil in wok and add crushed chiles. After adding a lot of water and salt, cook the noodles in the water mixture for about 15 minutes. Add chopped scallions and chicken bouillon cubes.
- French fries. Scrub potatoes and boil, covered with water. Chop scallion greens and cut potatoes into lengths. Fry in a small amount of oil with onions and curry.
- Vegetable curry – Mash up garlic and chili peppers. Cook rice. Heat up wok and oil. Put in cauliflower (can use any vegetable

combination), spices, curry powder, and boiled potatoes. Add water after a few minutes (about 2 cups). Cook. Serve with rice.
- Toast – layer bread slices in frying pan. Cook until toasted. Turn.
- Roasted corn. Put directly in the coals (no tin foil)
- Potato pancakes. Grate potatoes to mush. Add flour to a medium consistency. Spread over curved plate (hot and oiled). Cook on both sides. Serve with chili sauce (mashed-up chilis, garlic and onion stalks) and butter.
- Bread and chips. Mix flour, water, egg and unknown spices. Slice potatoes very thickly. Fry potatoes in oil and spices. Cover slice of bread in flour mixture. Fry.
- *Chapati.* Mix flour, water, baking powder and salt. Roll out thinly. Cut into circles (size of saucer). Cook in pan with a little oil. Serve with jam. (They should puff up a bit when put on the coals.)
- Chili sauce. Basically, this is mashed up chilis and a little water, served with all vegetables, for example, corn or potatoes.

The variety of food, in general, is limited. There is no meat (Buddhists will eat meat if it has been killed by someone else, but there was no meat, chicken, or fish in this household). Eggs, which I requested and Phuti was wonderful to produce, are not a primary part of the diet. The two girls loved the eggs; it was a treat for them. A great deal of time is spent preparing and storing food for the winter—putting beans, potatoes, and other vegetables into large, bronze pots. The preparation for vegetables such as potatoes, gourd squash, lima or pinto beans before storing them is simple: Mash potatoes and add chopped scallion greens, crumble, and spread out to dry in the sun for a day or two, then store. When using, mix with a little water and cook. This is especially good for *dal bhat*.

MY SHERPA VOCABULARY[40]
(A limited list, but utilized every day)

Apple – nusputi
Book – guh net ta
Comb – she sau
Corn – mucké
Ear – amjo
Eye – mik
Flour – sampa
Flute – lumoo
Fog – mukpaa
Good – lemu
Goodbye – khole phep (to someone going)
Good morning – tashi dele
Good night – khole zim
Hair – schruh
Head – gō
Hello – Tong boo
How do you say – Kang-si dela
I – nga
More – manga
No – mengbi
OK – las
Pen – ka lum
Pencil – pil-sheen
Please – thaakur
Quiet – ko simbu
Rain – chharwaa

---

40 Sherpa, Ang Phinjo, *Sherpa Nepali English*, Jeewan Printing Support Press, 1989.

Rice – drah
Run – dang nie dap
Sing – lu linggu
Skip – doo kangna dap
Sun - nyima
Tea (black) – chuhpika
Thank you - thuche
That is enough – langsum
Towel – roo mal
Walk/Go – daap
Wash (to) - tutu
Water – chhu
Where – khani
You – khyorong

And, necessary for the spider song:

Itsy-Bitsy – Tikpe
Spider - Bu
Waterspout - Kangbaa
Rain – Chharwaa
Sun - Nyima

AUTHOR'S NOTES

So much has changed in Nepal since 1999. At that time, the IMF eLibrary noted that, "Nepal's growth potential continues to be limited by an underdeveloped physical infrastructure, unskilled human resources, and poor institutional capacity. Economic growth has been insufficient to raise living standards and per capita income remains at $200. Almost 90 percent of the Nepali population live in rural areas and their incomes depend on subsistence farming."[41]

The trekking business in Nepal does indeed encourages much to grow and thrive. For example, in 2001, the landing strip at Lukla was paved; and in 2008, the airport was renamed in honor of Sherpa Tensing Norgay and Hillary, the first confirmed to have reached the summit of Mount Everest.

There was a devastating event, the Gorkha earthquake (magnitude of 7.8) in 2015. The Encyclopedia Britannica details the earthquake, "that struck near the city of Kathmandu in central Nepal on April 25, 2015. About 9,000 people were killed, many thousands more were injured, and more than 600,000 structures in Kathmandu and other nearby towns were either damaged or destroyed…. the earthquake also triggered an avalanche on Mount Everest that killed at least 19 climbers and stranded hundreds more at Everest Base Camp and at camps higher up the mountain. Those at the high camps were soon airlifted to Base Camp, and all the climbers either hiked off the mountain or were flown out to other locations."[42] Since that time, massive reconstruction to the

---

[41] International Monetary Fund, 1999, https://www.elibrary.imf.org/view/journals/002/1999/018/article-A001-en.xml.

[42] Rafferty, John P., "Nepal Earthquake of 2015," https://www.britannica.com/topic/Nepal-earthquake-of-2015.

infrastructure has taken place, for example the work that Pemba Sherpa has achieved in the Khumbu region. It is difficult to imagine the tragedy in the area that was such a dramatic backdrop to my months in Nepal.

In this story about those three months, I spoke about the difficulty of finding a Sherpa dictionary, one that could aid in my introduction to the country. As time elapsed in Sengma, the lack of communication became so complex that this deficit came to be the foundation for my isolation. My timing for visiting the Khumbu region was unfortunate for in 2023 there are many words written about the language, not to mention a myriad number of video sites to aid in learning the vocabulary and grammar. The Sherpa language is difficult as it is primarily a spoken language related to a Tibetan dialect, different from Nepali derived from Sanskrit. At birth, names are often given to the child according to the day of the week (for example, Pemba is Saturday). The name 'Sherpa' is a culture, a language, a people, a surname, and a name given to extraordinary climbers, guides, and porters—an incredible lineage. I would like to end with words, no doubt the most important, about the Sherpas.

Pemba Sherpa, in *Bridging Worlds*

"For centuries, Sherpas lived in relative isolation as farmers, herders, and traders. Because of its remoteness and inaccessibility, Khumbu remained virtually cut off from the outside world until the mid-1900s, when British climbers turned their attention to Nepal in their effort to summit Mount Everest. Ultimately, this spawned a climbing and trekking industry that would profoundly change the region and transform Sherpa culture. Roughly 3,000 Sherpas presently live in Khumbu, while another 30,000 inhabit small villages scattered throughout the mountains of eastern Nepal.... Contrary to the assumption of many, a Sherpa is not a porter or mountain guide. The word "sherpa" has been distorted by Westerners to mean a particular occupation in the climbing industry. But this is not accurate. To be a Sherpa is to be a member of an ethnic tribe that settled the Everest region of Nepal roughly 500 years ago, the first people to inhabit this part of the Himalaya. Beginning sometime in the early 1400s, a small group of Sherpa families began a migration from eastern Tibet that would eventually land them in the uninhabited Solo Khumbu region of Nepal. The name "Sherpa" speaks to these origins, translated from Tibetan to mean "People from the East." Four main clans, numbering perhaps fifty individuals in all, migrated from Kham in eastern Tibet, bringing with them the traditions and religion of Tibetan Buddhism. In subsequent years, they would be followed by other Sherpa clans coming from Tibet. Among the highest mountain dwellers on earth, Sherpa People today are known throughout the world as the fabled inhabitants of the Himalaya."[43]

---

[43] Sherpa, Pemba with James McVey, *Bridging Worlds, A Sherpa's Story*, Sherpa Publications, 2019

ACKNOWLEDGEMENTS

Twenty years past the events of 1999, remembering the particulars of the land and life of the Sherpa, I am regretful that much was forgotten. In writing a story about hiking the hills of Khumbu and how I lived, this is my best memory. To Pemba, Phuti, Chongba, Tshering and Dinesh, to whom I owe so much, it is my wish that you can remember with pleasure the events of this narrative.

Many friends have contributed to this story, some who will never know how much their contribution fortified me during those three months. I want to thank my son, Jamie Lewis, who lives his own adventure day after day, for his comments and continued encouragement; to Elissa Guralnick for reading the manuscript and adding so much to this story; to Maggie Speier and Roy Lewis for their suggestions and words of encouragement; to my friends Erika Eckert, Angela Freiburg and Mairi Dorman-Phaneuf for preventing the writing of this adventure to languish in a sea of self-pity; to Katherine Schimmel, for her always invaluable suggestions (along with the title of this book); to Summer Boggess, now living her life in Montana, for her treasured little book; to my cousin, Robert Stacy, for our decisive discussions over hot dogs in Washington Square Park; to Dan Sher, Gene Hayworth, Keith Waters, and Ron Stewart—four gentlemen who gave encouragement at just the right time; to the friends and students who wrote via email or letter to an address in Nepal that was not an address at all in the hopes that their missives would eventually arrive to the little hamlet that was Sengma; to Dr. Hart of Boulder for her life-saving elixirs; to Gelbu Goparma Sherpa of California for his Sherpa translations; to Dinesh and Tshering who appeared at just the right moment; and to Pemba Sherpa for orchestrating my visit to Khumbu, and importantly, for all he has done to make life easier for the Sherpa in that region. I would like to suggest that everyone read Pemba's story, *Bridging Worlds,* a beautiful book written with James McVey—essential reading for those interested in the true Sherpa culture. Thank you all.

REFERENCES

Anker, Daniel, ed. *The Vertical Arena*, Mountaineers Books, 2000.
Arnette, Alan, "What's in a name: Everest, Chomolungma, Sagarmartha?" 2020, https://www.alanarnette.com/blog/2020/12/14/whats-in-a-name-everest-chomolungma-sagarmatha/.
Barzini, Luigi, *The Italians*, Touchstone, 1996.
"Because it's there," Forbes Magazine, October 2001. https://www.forbes.com/global/2001/1029/060.html?sh=32d47b4c2080
Benavides, Angela, "One Dead, One Missing on Mera Peak," 2021, https://explorersweb.com/one-dead-one-missing-on-mera-peak.
Better Place Forests, "The Complete Guide to Buddhist burial practices and rituals," 2022, https://www.betterplaceforests.com/blog/articles/the-complete-guide-to-buddhist-burial-practices-and-rituals.
Clark, Andrew, *Pablo Casals and the Resurrection of Bach's Cello Suites*, Financial Times, October 19, 2007.
Dalai Lama XIV, *Freedom in Exile: The Autobiography of the Dalai Lama*, Harper Collins, 1990.
Dalai Lama XIV, *The Path to Bliss: A Practical Guide to Stages of Meditation*, Snow Lion Publications, 1991.
Dalai Lama XIV, *Kindness, Clarity, and Insight*, Snow Lion Newsletter, Translated and edited by Jeffrey Hopkins and Elizabeth Napper, Autumn 2002.
"Gaur – the tiger killer, https://thewebsiteofeverything.com/animals/mammals/Artiodactyla/Bovidae/Bos/Bos-frontalis.html.
Glyde, Judith, "Practice Perfectly, not Practice Makes Perfect," *Strings*, July 2012, No.207, 34.
Holmes, David Dale, "Understanding the Four Noble Truths and the Noble Eightfold Path," Buddhistdoor Global, July 19, 2021 https://www.buddhistdoor.net/features/understanding-the-four-noble-truths-and-walking-the-noble-eightfold-path/
International Monetary Fund, 1999, https://www.elibrary.imf.org/view/journals/002/1999/018/article-A001-en.xml.
Jeziorski, Andrzej, *Nepal suffers second fatal crash*, Flight Global, September 14, 1999.
Kemp, Allyssa, "Solfège Syllables & Kodály Hand Signals, 2021, https://eastsidemusic.com/solfege-syllables-kodaly-hand-signals/.

"London Bridge," English nursery rhyme, the earliest records of the rhyme in English are from the 17th century. https://en.wikipedia.org/wiki/London_Bridge_Is_Falling_Down.

McGuinness, Jamie, *Trekking in the Everest Region*, Trailblazer Publications, 1993.

Miyolangsangma," 2022, https://en.wikipedia.org/wiki/Miyolangsangma.

North, Arthur Walbridge, *Camp and Camino in Lower California*. New York: The Baker & Taylor Company, 1910, pp. 279–280.

"Patan Durbar Square," https://en.wikipedia.org/wiki/Patan_Durbar_Square.

"Patan: Tibetan Refuge Camp," https://www.raonline.ch/pages/np/visin/np_patan01g.html.

"Peaks of Rolwaling," Highland Expeditions, https://highlandexpeditions.com/peaks-of-rolwaling/.

Prince Nepali, https://www.youtube.com/watch?v=HzKO5CfF5nE.

Rafferty, John P., "Nepal Earthquake of 2015, https://www.britannica.com/topic/Nepal-earthquake-of-2015.

Sherpa, Ang Phinjo, *Sherpa Nepali English*, Jeewan Printing Support Press, 1989.

Sherpa, Pemba, with James McVey, *Bridging Worlds, A Sherpa's Story*, Sherpa Publications, 2019.

Sophocles, *Oedipus Rex*, translated by Dudley Fitts and Robert Fitzgerald, 1949, 1977, Harcourt, Inc.

Stewart-Brown, Charlie, "The Tibetan Buddhist Translation of Om Mani Padme Hum," 2022, https://indivyoga.com/the-meaning-of-om-mani-padme-hum-in-tibetan-buddhism/

Thurman, Robert, *The Tibetan Book of the Dead*, Penguin Random Books, 1993.

World Travel Family, "Golden Temple Nepal. Rat Temple in Kathmandu," https://worldtravelfamily.com/rat-temple-nepal. "Tenzing-Hillary Airport," Wikipedia, the Free Encyclopedia, https://en.wikipedia.org/wiki/Tenzing-Hillary_Airport

Wylie, Charles, "Everest, 1953", *Himalayan Journal*. 2018, https://en.wikipedia.org/wiki/Imja_Tse.

ABOUT THE AUTHOR

© Roy Lewis

JUDITH GLYDE was formerly Professor of cello and chamber music and Chair of the String faculty at the University of Colorado. A founding member of the Manhattan String Quartet in 1970, she left the Quartet at the end of the 1991-92 season to join the faculty at CU.

She performed as teacher and guest artist with festivals including the Fairbanks (AK) Summer Arts Festival, the Adriatic Chamber Music Festival (IT), the Australian Chamber Music Festival in Townsville (AUS), the Castleman Quartet Program and the Music and Performance Arts Program—a study abroad program in Florence, Italy. Ms. Glyde was formerly Director of the Winterschool program of the ACMF and often presented pre-concert lectures for the Boulder Philharmonic and the CU Artists Series.

Formerly Artist-in-Residence at Town Hall in New York City; Colgate University, New York; and at Grinnell College, Iowa, Ms. Glyde performed over 80 concerts a year with the Manhattan Quartet, appearing throughout the United States, Europe, Canada, Mexico, the former Soviet Union, and South America. Their discography includes over 25 recordings for labels such as Naxos, Sony, Koch, Newport Classics, and Centaur Records, including a set of six ESS.A.Y. compact discs featuring the 15 string quartets of Dmitri Shostakovich, the first recording of the complete cycle by an American quartet.

In 2014, after retiring from the University of Colorado Boulder, she moved to Florence, Italy to investigate a new interest in Renaissance History and Art. Judith was also integral, with pianist, Antonio Artese, in the establishment of a study abroad program for music students in Florence and Siena. In 2017, she moved to Greenwich Village, New York City where she is on the Boards of Forever Buffs NY (CU alumni) and the non-profit organization, Friends of Chigiana. In the spring of 2022, she was honored when presented with the Distinguished Alumni Award from the College of Music, University of Colorado Boulder.

And she actually did restore a ruin in Bonefro, Molise, Italy, with the help of her good friend, Luigi Pece.

Pemba climbing in Eldorado Canyon Park, Boulder

Swayambhunath, Kathmandu

The Lukla Airport, 1999

Crossing the Dudh Kosi, Tshering and Diel with the cello

My home in Sengma

Upper Floor

With Phuti and the girls

Bath time – Saturday night

In the lower field

Chaurikharka and Lukla as seen from Sengma

Phuti and me

Pasang, with her doll

Tika threshing wheat

Mani stones, Chaurikharka

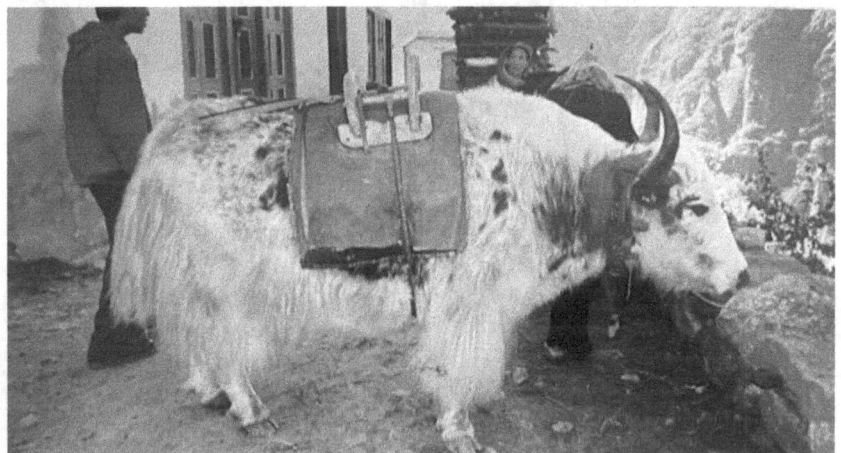

Yak, waiting patiently – Namche Bazaar

Luca Dawa, instrument maker

Porters – the load carriers

Hillary Bridge, on the way to Everest, 1999

Namche Bazaar in the Khumbu Valley, 1999

Everest, the Lhotse-Nuptse ridge and Ama Dablam, as seen from Everest View Lodge

The terraces of Nagarkot

Dinesh and Tshering

Patan Square, Lalitpur, Nepal, 1999

www.ingramcontent.com/pod-product-compliance
Lightning Source LLC
Chambersburg PA
CBHW011550070526
44585CB00023B/2524